developing tomorrow's managers today

developing tomorrow's managers today

FRANCIS W. DINSMORE

amacom

A DIVISION OF AMERICAN MANAGEMENT ASSOCIATIONS

Library of Congress Cataloging in Publication Data

Dinsmore, Francis W
    Developing tomorrow's managers today.

    1. Executives, Training of.   2. Executive ability.
3. Management.   I. Title.
HF5500.2.D55   658.4'07'124   75-9785
ISBN 0-8144-5387-2

A division of American Management Associations, New York.
All rights reserved. Printed in the United States of America.

First Printing

*To all those fellow managers
with whom I have enjoyed looking forward,
and to whom I shall always enjoy looking back*

preface

In the very practical world of business, it is not what you think, but what you know, that is important. And it is not just what you know that counts, but what you are able to do with what you know. This being so, it is surprising how many management development concepts and theories have been tried, on both an experimental and broad-scale basis, which were not based on knowledge and were not designed to accomplish measurable results.

The purpose of this book is to develop a better understanding of managers as they are and of how they can be changed to maximize what works best, not universally, but in one particular organizational environment—yours. The book has been designed to serve as a guide for all busy managers, but particularly those at the middle and higher levels. An attempt has therefore been made to keep it brief, concise, and to the point.

Some of the ideas contained herein may, hopefully, also serve to suggest new approaches to the many theorists in management behavior and organization development, so that they may in the future be of more practical help to those very practical people who perform the job of managing other managers.

Francis W. Dinsmore

contents

a realistic look at management development

1

Many people will tell you that an expert is one who knows a great deal about his subject. To this I would object that no one can ever know very much about his subject. I would much prefer the following definition: An expert is one who knows some of the worst mistakes which can be made in his subject and how to avoid them.

Niels Bohr

Finding a Program That Works

The seasoned manager appreciates that you must know *what works* in order to stay in business and that you must know *what works best* to be the leader in any particular field. In the general field of management development, a growing number of people are claiming to know a great deal about the subject, and many concepts have been developed on how managers should behave, or could behave, under certain conditions. In this number, however, there are few, if any, who can

1

tell a top executive that their concepts will *work* and, even more important, that they will *work best* for his particular organization.

There appears to be developing among many top executives a consciousness that they can cope with increasing pressures on themselves and their organizations only by having more individuals of character and ability in their management group. They see quite clearly the increasingly important part which must be played throughout the organization by managers capable of individual thinking and initiative. These executives have frequently seen the needs of their organizations outrunning the abilities of management, particularly in the middle and lower levels. They are becoming aware that what is required is an increasing dynamism—not just at the top, but at all management levels.

In looking for help in his management development program, the typical top executive is properly wary of some new theory claiming universal application and based upon ideas of how managers *should* behave (so that the theory will work). He needs a program based upon how his particular managers *do* and *can* behave— a program with a flexible approach in which he can custom-tailor changes and improvements to accomplish the specific goals *he* wants for *his* organization.

The top executive also tends to want any such program of change and improvement to be a gradual, step-by-step process rather than a revolutionary one. As in his other important business decisions, he automatically seeks to minimize the risk of unanticipated and unpleasant surprises.

Being a practical individual, the top executive wants, above all, a development program whose end result is not to make his managers *feel* better, but to have them *achieve* more. He recognizes, as a leader, the importance of setting high goals and motivating others to want and to work toward those goals. He appreciates that being a good manager really is a highly individual function, limited chiefly by the limitations of the individual manager's imagination. This function involves, he well knows, a never-ending process of learning to be a *better* manager—better in available resources, better in use of powers, and better in performance of responsibilities as measured by results. He is properly confident that any of his managers who improve in those areas will automatically *feel* better.

Our typical top executive most likely has experienced the following situation: The question of opening up a whole new area of business has come up for decision, and he asks his key subordinates, "Are we sure we can man it properly?" Together, they review how many really good managers there are throughout the organization, and it becomes clear that not one of his key people will admit to having enough of them. He notes nothing unnatural in this, since nobody likes to give up a good subordinate, and the request is sure to be made if someone admits to having more than his proper share.

On the other hand, the top executive reflects, this could also indicate that a number of managers are performing with something less than the desired efficiency and effectiveness. If so, this would be nothing new; he remembers the day long ago when he was interviewed for a starting position in this same company and the then top executive had said, "We never have enough good managers." The problem obviously had a long history and could hardly be considered one which required an

3

immediate solution. It was more in the nature of a lament, or corporate sigh, which nobody is really expected to do much about.

However, our top executive finds himself compelled to remark to his gathered subordinates, as he has done so often in the past, that a better job must be done by those responsible for recruiting. It is obvious, he says, that they just are not bringing enough really high-potential individuals into the management development ranks.

All those present quickly agree that this certainly is essential. Some, however, privately recall past recruitment, in what were then considered vintage recruiting years, which didn't seem to help all that much a few years later. They know the real answer must lie somewhere else. They also know the futility, and appreciate the danger, of making the issue a problem without having a possible solution to propose simultaneously. And none is aware of any such solution. Furthermore, within a few minutes after the meeting breaks up, all will immediately be engulfed in numerous other pressing problems which they *can* do something about.

Recognizing the Problem

The typical manager is reasonably content, though occasionally unhappy, with his management organization as it exists. He is furthermore pleased that his organization's use of its people resources is not subject to the same objective scrutiny applied to most other parts of his operations.

The people-handling area, he knows, is much less frequently and less thoroughly audited and is less subject to objective measurement by individuals in departments outside his direct control. He will probably be required to operate according to an established manpower authorization and an organization chart and will be asked to comment on an occasional turnover report prepared by the personnel department. Otherwise he will simply be asked once, or maybe a few times, per year to give an opinion on how his people are doing.

If the operations are going well and all the figures compiled on a regular basis reflect what appears to be a healthy business, no red flags are going to pop up and no embarrassing questions are going to arise with regard to that manager's people handling. It is assumed that the purpose of people is to make the numbers come out right. Of course, if the numbers don't come out right, the manager will probably be asked for an opinion about the people responsible, but there is little in the way of factual evidence, and certainly no magic numbers, to gainsay his opinion. As a manager, he can derive a warm feeling of comfort from the realization that the people-handling area is the one part of his operations over which he continues to retain unilateral control.

Recognition of a problem is certainly the first step toward its solution. But an internally generated problem which is not forced to the forefront by outward circumstance is usually not formally recognized to exist— unless a possible solution is available. With recognition of the problem thus virtually squelched, the other steps in management development are unlikely to be taken. And even when, occasionally, they are taken, they do not produce measurable results. The primary reason for this is that successful managerial experience is seldom recorded except to the extent to which it is reflected in a company's general policies, principles, and procedures.

There has, of course, been no dearth of writings on management development by academicians and theorists. However, those people have helped mostly to define the problems. There has been no way for them to learn how organizations really work in situations where the individuals involved, as well as the factors working on those individuals, are varied and constantly changing. As a result, none of the various theories and systems applied to date has had much measurable effect on the actual practices of managers as they go about their job of controlling and measuring the performance of subordinate managers. The importance of this shortcoming cannot be exaggerated, since it is only improved managerial practices which can result in greater levels of achievement for individual managers and for the organization as a whole.

Establishing the Program's Goals

The first step in any program for change and improvement in managerial practices is to establish three very specific goals, all of which are important:

1. To provide a broader base of highly competent managers from whom selection can be made for positions of highest responsibility.

2. To provide greater assurance that all managerial positions at all levels are filled with individuals competent to help in moving the business ahead.

3. To provide a working environment which ensures for each individual manager greater resources for his continuing growth, and increased opportunity to use his powers and to achieve his full potential.

Any program developed in support of these objectives must be realistically based upon a clear understanding of the requirements of the individual manager and the total organization. Also, it must include methods for capitalizing fully on the organization's managerial experience with regard to *what works best.*

To be truly successful, a management development program must also face head on, and provide a procedure for resolving, a heretofore unresolved problem: how to measure and evaluate the relative effectiveness of each manager in a more meaningful and objective manner. The very limited ability to measure individual managerial performance objectively at various levels in the organization has, in the past, resulted in overemphasis on subjective evaluations.

It cannot be denied that the management of managers may long continue to be more of an art than a science. The scientific approach tends to be based on rather methodical analytical processes designed to provide answers to problems which can be very specifically defined. Most problems concerning managers, to the contrary, do not lend themselves readily to such a scientific approach. Such problems must be handled with a considerable amount of flexibility and imagination and with recognition that what works for one manager may not work equally well, or at all, for another.

The crux of the measurement problem obviously is this: How can sufficient objectivity be obtained without the use of the purely scientific approach? Another matter for consideration is the determination of those factors whose measurement will yield greater control of managerial performance. Since such performance is always changing, for better or worse, the careful selection of those factors to be measured and eventually controlled must be considered of the greatest importance.

It should be recognized from the beginning that any program with such ambitious objectives for a particular organization, or a cohesive part of it, will not be easy. It will require planning, coordination, and the continuing effort of each manager and a planned overall control from the top.

All too frequently in the past, the development of managers has been accepted as meaning simply maximum effort on the part of the individual to develop and to advance himself. It has been assumed that in such a working environment the cream will float to the top, and indeed this often appears to be true. For the corporation interested exclusively in maintaining a limited supply of top managers, this one-dimensional approach may have proved to be reasonably satisfactory. However, the number of organizations which can afford such a limited approach to the development of management talent is growing smaller each year.

A management development program must be realistic and directly relevant to the specific needs of each top manager with respect to his organization. The program must remain flexible so that it can be custom-tailored to what any top manager wants in order to meet these needs. In discovering and expanding the practices that work best, it may well be found initially desirable to select for a depth study a single important factor which could have a big payoff. For example, in sales, such a factor might be the development of the best way of handling the customer who says, "No, I don't need any"; in advertising, it might be a study of patterns in copy which are related to improved sales for particular types of products; in manufacturing, a study of the best way to obtain and maintain a two-way communication between management and labor; in a staff department, the determination of the most essential service being provided and how it can be made even more useful to its recipients.

A program of specific and continuing effort to develop, at all levels, more managers who are high achievers by exposing them to what works best will create a dynamic environment—the kind of environment for people and ideas upon which the consistent growth and profit of any organization depends.

In the following chapters a way of thinking is developed about the managerial process which can be directly translated into a way of doing. The subject of management development is explored from a manager's viewpoint, that is, in terms of determining what needs to be done, deciding how to do it, and seeing that it gets done.

the manager
as an individual

2

*The scientist, the chemist, the physicist, the engineer,
have taught us to accept imaginative thinking and to lay
aside our instinctive reaction that "it can't be done."
We need this kind of thinking in our development of
human talents. We need it badly and soon. We need the
creative imagination, the boldness, the refusal to accept
the obvious or to recognize the "impossible." Our
problems are big; they need big solutions which will
deserve and require the best thoughts of all of us.*

Neil McElroy

Individuality and the Potential Manager

Business organizations are dependent to a large extent
upon the colleges and universities for an annual crop of
potential managers. Businessmen would do well to
follow the oft-quoted example of the good farmer who,
being dependent upon the condition of his soil for the
success of his crops, does his best to nurture that soil.
This is particularly true nowadays, when so much of the
college crop seems to go through periodic cycles of
questioning whether it wants to devote its life to busi-

ness, or even questions seriously the viability of the whole system. Some of these questions are reasonable and some not so reasonable, but it is becoming increasingly important for business to provide a more carefully considered "corporationale," which will help to answer at least some of the more important and insistent questions.

One of the most basic campus concerns about business involves individuality. You may or may not like the form of expression this sometimes assumes. But like it or not, you cannot talk for a minute with a student, whether undergraduate or candidate for M.B.A., without quickly sensing the great importance he or she attaches to being an individual. It takes only another minute to uncover a very basic worry about how much individual identity will have to be sacrificed if he or she goes to work in a business organization, particularly a large corporation.

Students also tend, for the most part, to be conscious only of the worst examples of bad business practices from the past. They simply are not being informed about the increasingly important role of the individual in the success of any modern, dynamic corporation. They seem to be almost totally unaware that the ability of managers to work together as individuals in an efficient and effective organizational framework has been developed in business to a much higher level than in most other parts of our highly organized society. The same cannot be said for the typical business structures of most other countries. In fact, the author shares with others who have worked outside the United States a strong feeling that the thing which most sets American businesses apart from foreign businesses is not corporate structure or technical competence. Rather, it is what

11

has been described as the peculiarly American ability of individuals to work creatively with other individuals within a complex organizational framework. Despite the complexity of the organization, there is considerable freedom for individual initiative at many levels.

It may be wrong to refer to this ability as uniquely American, since it is also frequently observed in international Canadian and Australian operations. In fact, it seems to be most prevalent among the younger nations and, generally, in situations of rapid growth which require the maximum number of new initiatives.

In any event, individual initiative and creativity are much less apparent in the generally more structured and authoritarian organization typical of Great Britain and much of Europe. Although many changes are taking place over there, it is still not uncommon to find a giant publicly owned corporation dominated by one individual and three or four subordinates, in a manner reminiscent of the family enterprise in the United States. In such an organization, that small group of executives gathers to discuss what they think, after which the top man makes his decision and the word goes down to the troops. What little middle management exists is limited to seeing that orders are carried out.

Of course, this system works, at least well enough for the organization to remain in business most of the time—but seldom well enough for it to obtain and maintain a position of leadership. It might be said that the campus view of the corporate world tends to be an exaggerated composite of this old-fashioned daguerreotype and a picture of an impersonal giant. It is therefore not surprising to find on most campuses little or no appreciation of what business today is all about, and little or no knowledge of the many important positions between the top and the bottom in which individuals play so many interesting and important parts.

This is a dangerous breach of understanding, which some might be tempted to call a gap. However, the word "gape" might be better suited. The dictionary defines "gape" as "an open-mouthed stare; hence a state of wonder." There appear to be entirely too many people on today's campuses with the "organization gapes." To a certain degree, of course, this has always been true, but it must be remembered that in former days there were far fewer alternative career options available to those on campus who professed little or no interest in business.

The reasons for the organization gapes are many and varied, but those about which something can be done certainly include the following:

1. The business community is providing practically no real information about, or insight into, the process of managerial control. Results-oriented pragmatist that he is, and rightly so, the successful businessman has been universally noted for his lack of interest in what might be called the philosophy of business. Despite his free use of the analytical process, he has looked upon any form of self-analysis as an indication of "academic thinking," which is in itself deserving of severe opprobrium.

2. Any understanding which has existed between business and academia has been undermined in recent years by the technological explosion. Not only has that phenomenon caused changes in the products and services of business, but it has necessitated many less obvious changes—in the ways managers work together, as well as in practices and organizational structure. As a result, it

has become more difficult for academic minds to analyze and understand the business scene today. Unfortunately, the most brilliant academicians are no different from the rest of us in that they distrust what they do not understand.

3. Academic training places maximum emphasis on the performance of individuals acting alone. For most of the period from elementary school through college, it is more a question of how much can be soaked up rather than how much can be wrung out. Schools and colleges are simply not designed for the purpose of helping students to learn how to work effectively with others in an organizational framework. Of course, there is nothing *new* about this, and for that reason if for no other, it is probably subject to suspicion.

Even in the best graduate schools of business, you have only to ask the dean or one of the professors to identify those students who will most likely become the most successful managers. They readily admit that this is impossible to do, but they can identify those who seem to be the "smartest." This is a matter for concern since most of the goals generally accepted by our highly organized society—and vociferously expressed on campus—can be achieved only within some organizational framework and not by individuals acting alone. It would seem that the students are the first to be awakening to this and that they have at least one legitimate basis for complaining that their studies are not sufficiently relevant to the times.

Businessmen should find encouragement in that development, as well as in the increasing desire of students to play a more active part in managing the affairs of their colleges and universities. In practice, such management experience could be quite valuable in teaching the students to work constructively within an organization. Like students, lawyers frequently tend to be unpracticed in how to work effectively with others within a complex organizational structure. It is worth noting that the Age of Protest was started by students, and the Age of the Adversary by lawyers.

To offset students' lack of understanding about business, companies have relied largely upon recruiting literature. Much of this is carefully prepared and makes even the annual report look shabby by comparison. Unfortunately, to any but the most naive student, most of this recruiting literature sounds alike. Also, students are understandably skeptical, having taken too many courses which turned out to be barely recognizable in terms of their descriptions in the course prospectus. The more mature student wants, therefore, to know what the actual business practices are. At this point, it might be fair to say that if most companies actually lived up to their recruiting literature, the applicants would be knocking down their doors.

Here is a suggestion for the next time you, as a manager, are trying to interest a student in joining your organization: Start by agreeing with him or her that simply administering an established business could be pretty boring. Talk about this for a bit, taking advantage of the opportunity to amplify the basic difference between an administrator, who carries out the ideas of others, and a manager, whose most important job is to figure out what needs to be done in the first place.

Give the student examples of how you and other managers actually operate in facing unusual and difficult situations. You may be surprised to see how quickly the mask of doubt and suspicion is replaced by a light in his eyes, an increased interest, and an awareness that being a successful manager is going to require him to be a bigger individual than he now is, or even has imagined he could be.

The mature student generally accepts the fact that success in almost any field of endeavor comes only with enthusiasm and the kind of contribution which can be made because the work captures the imagination. However, he frequently has a stereotyped picture of the personal characteristics and abilities needed to succeed in business. With little prior experience, he has a shallow basis on which to decide whether the working environment in a particular company will satisfy his wants and further the development of the characteristics and abilities he will need.

The fault for this lies not with the student, but with business, which must assume responsibility for doing a better job of communicating with him. The best business representative to do this is frequently a young and successful manager who himself is only a few years out of college. One of the good things about the complexity of business today is that there really is a tremendous number of responsible positions for younger managers which provide above-average compensation and sources of satisfaction for those who can make the required contribution.

The word "contribution" should be emphasized. If there is an almost universal weakness in students' thinking, it is their overemphasis on things they find or might find *interesting,* and lack of emphasis on their *contribution.* The student will listen when a young manager points out that a contribution carries with it a sense of accomplishment and that it is this sense of accomplishment which provides the real satisfaction and the basis for increased interest.

The validity of this point is supported by the experience of businesses which have experimented with summer jobs for potential management trainees. In these programs designed to introduce students, including first-year M.B.A.'s, to managerial responsibilities, it has frequently been found that even a 10- or 12-week introduction can actually decrease interest and enthusiasm unless the summer trainee has an opportunity to make a real contribution.

Individuality and the Manager

There are many aspects of the manager's job which emphasize the importance of individual distinctiveness. Probably none is more central than the ability to communicate. Communication means different things to different people. It is universally accepted to include the ability to express oneself clearly, concisely, and to the point in both written and oral forms. In its best sense it includes the ability to listen as well as to talk, and to understand as well as to make oneself understood.

Listening to, and really trying to understand, another's point of view is something for which there is precious little time in a busy manager's day. It is hard, however, to argue with the behavioral scientists who state that the chances of influencing others are much better if those others feel they have a chance, at least sometimes, to influence you. In other words, communication automatically includes a knowledge, and appreciation, of the point of view and feelings of others. Delegation is another act which can be performed intelligently only when based upon a reasonably good understanding of the other individual—that is, upon a knowledge of the strengths and weaknesses of the person to whom responsibility or authority is being given.

It is also important that a manager have a proper awareness of his own individuality. The better the manager evaluates his personal abilities and understands his own requirements in terms of money, status, and opportunity at various stages in his career, the better his chances of satisfying those needs. This is largely because the manager, in functioning at any level, must be able to find his own way in assuming responsibility and authority as well as in having feasible ideas and coordinating his actions with others.

Job descriptions may serve some purpose for administrators, but for managers they are properly scorned in most good business organizations. Unfortunately, this is sometimes wrongly interpreted as meaning that a superior should do nothing at all to inform his subordinates on what is expected of them. This can result in much unnecessary confusion and conflict.

A manager must also feel a very personal sense of responsibility not only for his own work, but for the work of others which can affect the results of his work. In most good business organizations there is a deliberate attempt to pinpoint one individual who will be primarily responsible for achieving a specific desired objective.

A major factor which is making the exercise of managerial responsibility more individual is the necessity for more experts in more areas of the business. This has tended to increase the responsibilities of a larger number of managers whose authority comes not from position, but from their personally knowing more about a given area than anybody else in the organization.

No organization can long exist without leadership, as well as authority and controls. Leadership is very distinctly individual. The leader is one who will challenge the accepted way as only the person of character with his own way of thinking and sense of integrity can do. Likewise, the pressures which constantly develop within an organization all end up pointing at individuals. From these pressures come priorities, which are all established by individual reactions to the pressures.

Nobody knows better than the manager who is a leader that, whether selling a proposition up the line or motivating others down the line to certain goals, it is best to know as individuals the people you are trying to influence. As in any other form of selling, it is essential to know what really interests the individual to whom you are making a proposition. Any group's effectiveness will usually vary directly with the ability of its leader to influence others outside of the group.

Sometimes it is said too glibly that decision making is becoming largely a group process. This is not literally so, and the statement can be misleading. It may be quite true that more and more people are becoming regularly involved in the process by which decisions are made, in input on alternatives, in risk assessment, and in the clearance process.

However, decision making involves certain key steps which can generally be best performed by one person charged with primary responsibility in the area of decision. This manager usually establishes the original reason why a decision is needed, what it is that he desires to have happen. It is also he who is in the best position to choose among various alternative actions designed to achieve the desired results and he who must follow through in seeing that all those involved in the actions properly carry out their assigned responsibilities.

It is thus seen that decision is closely related to initiative, than which nothing is more important in most organizations. A sound, practicable proposal to change an accepted practice, or to take a new direction, inevitably is initiated by someone who can think for himself. No organization has enough of such individuals.

A corporation does not exist apart as an impersonal entity. What the company *is* results directly from what each manager *does.* The basic character of the company is, likewise, the direct result of how they do it. Individual initiative in all managers is, therefore, something which must be carefully nurtured and controlled in the best interests of the organization as a whole.

Basic Types of Managers

Before proceeding any further, it might be timely to look briefly at managers as they actually are in their relations with other managers, since, to be effective, any management development program must deal with individuals as they are rather than as they should be. The ways in which managers work with their subordinates are found, quite naturally, to vary considerably in any organization. Those relationships are probably the area which has the greatest effect upon achievement level.

Experience would suggest that managers can be grouped, for the sake of simplicity, into three basic types—the crap shooter, the poker player, and the bridge player. Since business is a game of chance and risk, this is not too surprising.

The crap shooter is a manager who has what might be

called the "audiovisceral" approach to his subordinates. This is a gut feeling about them which is either generally favorable or unfavorable. If it is favorable, he will grant a considerable amount of freedom to the subordinate—in effect, giving him his turn with the dice. However, the minute fortune ceases to smile on the subordinate, the manager will immediately start placing bets against him. The crap shooter in business is a great believer in the chance theory of success. This results in an unwillingness or inability to judge performance on any basis other than the very pragmatic one of immediate results. Subordinates of such crap shooters are frequently found to "need a new pair of shoes."

The poker player is another gambler at heart. He is also a great believer in the odds, which, because of his superior position, always are arranged to favor him. The poker player is out to beat everybody, not just his subordinates, by playing his cards very close to his vest. His primary aim is to win the maximum number of hands on a bluff which gets the others to throw in their hands without forcing him to expose his. The poker player takes his clues entirely from the strength of the cards he holds, and his purpose is to seem smarter than anybody else. Everybody in the game—that is, within the organization—is a direct competitor, and he will happily take his best friend to the cleaners.

Both the crap shooter and the poker player usually belong to what might be called the authoritarian school. Both also tend to think of people in terms of opposite qualities, or characteristics that are mutually exclusive; to have one quality, it is necessary to sacrifice the other. To this way of thinking, initiative and aggressiveness go together and cannot coexist with listening to others or caring about their needs or wants. Furthermore, since the crap shooter and poker player have progressed on the basis of their ability as such they will always opt for the game they know best. They will resist attempts to change the rules of the game or any suggestion for a different kind of game.

The bridge player, if he is any good, is also a gambler, but he is most interested in assessing risks. He differs fundamentally from the crap shooter and the poker player in that his game depends on having a partner who understands the same conventions. Furthermore, he must share information with his partner in arriving at an agreed contract, or objective, with each hand that is dealt. His duty to his partner, or team, then becomes making or exceeding the contract. He can be, and usually is, just as competitive as the other two types but recognizes that he can't play the game alone. He particularly appreciates a really able partner.

The bridge player is on the increase among management types and is most frequently found with those who practice, in one form or another, the system of management by objectives—objectives which are jointly arrived at even though usually decided upon by the partner with the stronger hand.

All three types can be found in varying forms at all levels in most organizations. In their lower forms, the crap shooter and the poker player are not above loading the dice or stacking the deck. The only objective for them is to win and win big. The bridge player may renege or play from the wrong hand if not watched carefully, but it is mostly the game itself and the open competition with other keen minds which grasp his imagination and hold his interest.

The authority of position, whereby one individual has authority over another because of the linear construction of the organization chart, is not only the most obvious form of authority, but probably the most abused—particularly at lower and middle management levels. It is too frequently associated with power *over other people,* rather than *over situations,* and can be exercised quite arbitrarily. This kind of position authority can result in the development of managers who are authoritarians or autocrats.

The autocrat in his purest form must be considered today to be an anachronism who is still thinking in terms of the boss-worker environment of yesteryear, and handles his subordinate managers accordingly. He can be quickly recognized by his belief that although there may be two sides to every question, there can be only one answer. Quite frequently he will take pride in thinking "only business" and will be unable to make the nice distinction between "only business" and "all business," or to visualize the ways in which the wants and needs of the individual and the organization can be mutualized to the benefit of both.

The true autocrat has a great faith in himself and generally displays very little confidence in subordinates; he will often be arbitrary and autocratic, simply to establish clearly who is boss.

The authoritarian, who tends to be an autocrat who has seen the light, is most frequently found in an organization where the style of leadership is one which expects a minimum of initiative from the middle and lower levels of management. The authoritarian is generally found in higher management ranks, where he often surrounds himself with myriad rules and procedures which he considers essential to his personal execution of responsibilities.

Behavioral scientists have properly noted that the authoritarian who is in tune with the organization's general style of leadership does not create any great problems for a subordinate, but when his existence is atypical, he can be the source of much unnecessary conflict. The potential weakness, of course, of any too consistently authoritarian or autocratic manager is that he may fail in securing from others the coordination and enthusiastic cooperation needed to achieve a difficult objective. This will frequently happen because the others, particularly if not immediate subordinates, have no clear understanding of what is wanted and how they are to share in the responsibility, so they wait to be told.

Upward Orientation and Achievement

It would be wrong to mention the problems which can develop between superior and subordinate without calling attention to the three-way orientation which the achiever usually has with respect to others in the organization. It will frequently be found that the most effective managers are those who have what might be called upward orientation, in addition to their orientation downward to subordinates and sideways to their peers at the same general level in other functional areas.

It might even be fair to state that no matter how effective a manager may be with those beneath him and at the same level, his ability to advance either himself or the business will be severely curtailed if he is not upwardly oriented. In the briefest terms this means a conscious effort to know and understand those above him in the organization and to think at their level when the need arises. It also means an ability to grasp what is wanted without having it spelled out; this is sometimes described as a sense of the situation and at other times as an ability to make the boss look good. Some managers seem to have a natural and uncanny ability in this direction, others acquire it only after considerable effort, and still others never do achieve it.

Upward orientation will be dealt with in more detail in subsequent chapters. Simply because it is so important to the manager's ability to raise his achievement level, it should receive major attention in any management development program.

the manager and management 3

People ask the difference between a leader and a boss.
The leader works in the open and the boss in covert.
The leader leads and the boss drives.

T. Roosevelt

Management: Science or Art?

It might be proper to introduce this section by recognizing that there are undoubtedly some companies in which the practice of management is still at a stage that is unacceptable to either those who consider management a science or those who consider it an art. Reference here is made to companies which do not recognize the importance of the individual and tend to treat all employees as a commodity, whether they be hourly, clerical, or managerial.

The management of managers in such companies may bear a close resemblance to horticulture or animal husbandry. In the management of plants, the terms most frequently used are "force," "transplant," "thin," and "prune." In the management of animals, the corresponding terms are "drive," "harness," "groom," "milk," and "shear." Policies in such companies generally are based upon the carrot and the stick and do not keep up very well with the changes that are taking place except when forced to do so by external circumstances, such as the actions of a union. Top executives in such companies who are not concerned about their management development policies should, perhaps, recognize the writing on the wall: In the schools nowadays it is not the janitors who are striking, but the teachers.

Even in the more enlightened companies, which fortunately are in the majority today, it is natural for top managers to view any proposed change in policy as a potential threat. This creates a tendency to hold on to policies even after they have become outmoded, particularly policies dealing with managerial behavior. Here there is always a certain amount of reassurance in pretending that things are really not all that different. A frequently heard, but superficial, argument is that human nature doesn't change, so why shouldn't managerial policies remain the same?

It is a fact, however, that in most organizations a growing number of managers, particularly in the lower and middle ranks, feel that, despite all the talk, the organizational environment is not designed to encourage the realization of their true and full potential as managers. It is also a fact that more and more top executives are coming to realize that they must change that environment or be shortchanged by a less efficient, less effective total effort from their management group. We have, then, a situation in which all parties have reasons for being less than happy with the situation as it exists. This has brought onto the stage the management scientists and behavioral scientists who, in increasing numbers, are challenging those who believe in management as an art.

Many believers in management as an art basically are saying that management is something which one cannot be taught but must simply learn for himself. The financial rewards alone are considered sufficiently great that any person with the necessary drive and ability will do just that. This is the one-dimensional approach referred to previously, where interest is centered almost entirely on separating the cream from the top. It is not surprising to find this simplistic approach to management as an art most prevalent among those in the higher ranks of management, since it is an automatic ego massager. Some will even go so far as to say that managing simply means leadership and "leadership is a birthright."

The trouble with this kind of thinking applied to business management is that there is just enough truth in it to mislead. In politics, for example, Winston Churchill is certainly accepted as one of the great political leaders of the twentieth century, and many might say that for him leadership was a birthright. However, it should be remembered that nobody particularly wanted his leadership until World War II, when he was well into his sixties, and that he was rejected immediately following the war's end. In his 90 years, he was a brilliant leader for six. If it had not been for the war, he might never have been remembered as a leader at all.

In a way, this points up the need to remind ourselves

continually that in the business world being a good manager means being a *consistently* good manager and involves two separate and distinct sets of abilities. One set of abilities tends primarily to advance the self, and the other tends mostly to advance the business. People have these two sets of basic management abilities in varying combinations. Another way of saying this is that some managers tend more to create and contribute, and others to take and use.

The individual who tends to take and use is generally found to be particularly adept at mastering the system and finding ways to make the system work for him, rather than fighting it. Part of his strategy for self-advancement calls for finding ways to associate himself with success. He is also "too busy with more important things" to pay much attention to problem areas which hold the potential danger of association with failure. He is not without ability to advance the business but husbands his creative abilities and concentrates his contribution in one or two areas where he is naturally strong.

On the other hand, the manager who tends to create and contribute seems generally to be slower in learning to make the system work for him, but learn he must if he is to maximize his ability to contribute.

In the modern, complex organization where the leadership style is one of viewing management development as the simple art of self-advancement, certain characteristics and abilities associated with self-advancement often tend to become overemphasized. In such an environment it is quite easy for a staff group working closely with a line group to fall into the trap of thinking that the attributes and abilities needed for the two different responsibilities are the same.

For example, the primary objective of the staff group may be to provide essentially creative thinking in a specialized area, such as sales promotion. The manager of the staff group may have a certain false pride or be concerned about appearing to be in any way different from, and therefore inferior to, the line manager. As a result, he tries to manage his staff group as though it were a line group, failing to recognize the different combination of abilities his people require in order to achieve their more specialized objective. The most creative member of the group may then find himself transferred to another area of the business, because his superior feels that he lacks the desired "executive leadership qualities," which in fact have no effect upon that member's contribution.

In the same manner it is not so unusual to observe a younger manager make rapid advancement by impressing the right people with his "leadership qualities" even though his direct contributions in the way of practical ideas that have advanced the business are very hard to find.

There is no question that good management is an art requiring expertness based on specific talents and even an occasional touch of genius or good luck. The point being made is that it can be dangerous to overemphasize throughout an organization the abilities associated with advancing the self at the expense of those associated with advancing the business.

As for the proponents of scientific management, they have accomplished much in the restructuring of organizations, in operations research, and in production techniques, including data processing. However, neither they nor the behavioral scientists have, to date, been able to affect significantly the thinking of higher-level managers about managerial behavior or the development of better managers.

The true believers in the scientific approach to managerial behavior are seldom found among top executives or line managers, but rather in academic circles and certain staff groups, including management consultants. These proponents are convinced that, by studying cause and effect with scientific analysis, they can develop pertinent principles about human behavior. They believe that those principles, if broadly applied by the managers, would result in a more effective organization.

Unfortunately, when applied to managerial behavior, the five steps in the scientific approach (definition, analysis, measurement, experiment, and proof) have too frequently ended up short of proof. The behavior of individuals, even in small groups, has proven to be too complicated and too changeable, so that in the long run the scientific approach tends to break down.

It can be argued convincingly that there just isn't enough knowledge, and probably never will be, about human behavior in management situations to permit development of principles or theories with any chance of universal application. Opponents believe that the scientific method applied to managerial behavior is worthless, because the study of cause and effect requires controlled conditions such as can exist only in a laboratory. In real-life business situations the relationships among the individuals being studied are forever changing, sometimes rapidly.

Particularly in their attempts to predict behavior, the scientific school theorists have erred many times because they fail to recognize or accept the real behavior of individuals in an organization and the extent to which even one person's behavior may vary in different situations—or even in seemingly similar situations. Although it may be possible to predict with reasonable accuracy how a particular manager will react in a specific situation, this ability to predict will not derive from any general theory but only from a real understanding of that individual.

Since the ability to predict is the greater part of the ability to control, the theorists can't be blamed for trying to reduce the interrelationships of managers to generalizations, theories, laws, rules, and the like. The trouble is that the managerial theorists, like so many economic theorists, tend to disregard anything that does not fit their theory. This is something that neither the money manager nor the people manager can afford to do. The insistence on orderliness and logic by the theorists is what turns off the line manager, who must learn to live with confusion just short of chaos. He must cope with people and situations as they are, and not as they should be.

The art and science schools of thought share a few common faults. Both have proved to be much more capable of identifying problems than of developing lasting solutions. Both have also tended to oversimplify the personal element in the equation. The art believer feels that a little scientific management applied to organizational structure and control procedures can be combined with authority and discipline to keep the entire process quite simple. The scientific proponent oversimplifies by exaggerating his knowledge of behavior and by artificially minimizing the number and variety of behavioral reactions so that certain factors can be isolated and examined as they would be in a laboratory.

Thinkers and Doers

Higher-level executives are almost always practical realists. The failure of the theorists to capture the minds of these executives is therefore not surprising. It results directly from the failure to come up with ways of measuring behavior patterns which can be meaningfully applied in specific situations. Any particular top executive may find himself intrigued by some of the innovative experiments which have been developed. But he will usually demand proof of effectiveness, knowing he would be foolish to permit the opinions and judgment of others to outweigh his own. The most predictable thing about a top executive is that he isn't much interested in what you *think;* he is interested only in what you *know.*

A further handicap to effective communication between thinkers and doers lies in the fact that most of the thinkers have never been doers and vice versa. It is the most natural thing in the world for a top executive to believe strongly in the basic code of managerial behavior which got him to the top. It is also natural for the ambitious manager on the way up to use successful superiors as models, and for a leader to choose as his replacement or right-hand man someone who seems to think and act much like himself. In this way, particular practices tend to become self-perpetuating, whether they are still relevant or not.

It becomes natural and too easy for a top executive to relax behind a complacent attitude of "prove it" whenever faced with proposed changes in the handling of managers in his organization. But before doing so, he might do well to examine at regular intervals the gaps that may be developing between policy and practice and, in particular, to find out what is going on in his organization at the lower levels of management.

It is undoubtedly true that very little in the way of real improvement can be made in an organization without the full cooperation and support of top management. But in the lower levels of management and among staff groups in many organizations today, there is a constant effort being made to change the behavioral practices of managers.

This effort, initiated at the bottom and directed upward, is probably more widespread than many top managers are aware. It poses a potential danger of serious proportions. It can result in raising expectation levels unrealistically. This in itself could be sufficient reason for all top managers to take an increased interest in any management development experiments which may be going on within their organization. However, there are at least three other very good reasons for this increased interest:

1. Even in the best-managed companies, there is a serious waste of individual potential. This is more important now than it has been in the past, because the complexities of business are increasing geometrically and creating a need for more and more good, feasible ideas at all levels, but particularly in the middle and lower management levels.

2. The beliefs, values, and habits which are being brought into management ranks today are quite different from those of even five years ago, and will continue to change. These new attitudes stem in part from the fact that a growing share of managerial positions is now held by members of minority groups, such as nonwhites and females.

Some may claim that these beliefs and habits will soon be modified, as in the past, by the policies, procedures, rules, and working discipline of the organization. However, any top manager who takes a good, hard look may find that the gap between what is going on and what should be going on is greater than he thinks. There is, of necessity, more peer group activity and interaction with others at the same level in other parts of the business. As a result, practices develop which, though perhaps not distinctly undesirable, may have a long-term effect on managerial behavior patterns quite the opposite of what the top executive is seeking for his organization.

3. In most of the larger corporations, as well as many smaller ones, a number of so-called experiments in managerial behavior have been attempted in the last few years in various parts of the organization. These include sensitivity training, T groups, grids, group dynamics, and other quasi- or pseudopsychological approaches. Any top manager who takes the time to probe more deeply may make a surprising discovery: These approaches are often quite broad-scale and cost a good deal in time and money, with little or no measurable effect upon the total output or effectiveness of the individual managers or groups involved. This occurs despite the fact that at the time of the experiments many participants say they think them helpful.

This failure of the analysts and theorists of behavioral science to provide the management doers with any meaningful measurements of the practical effectiveness of their many experiments is itself a subject worthy of some analysis. Available evidence would seem to indicate that there are several basic reasons for this failure:

1. In most instances the objectives of the experiment

are not clearly defined or spelled out and no means is provided by which results can be measured against these objectives.

2. Too frequently the objectives are really just to learn more about managerial behavior, even when the stated objectives are much broader. On that narrow basis such programs could not be justified. In some such instances, it may even be thought that the program will not do much actual good, but that it will at least be a neutralizer in indicating that the company is not automatically opposed to change.

3. Experiments of this type usually are based on general theories or concepts which are thought to have application to all types and levels of management throughout the organization. As a result, they are applied too broadly without regard to the specific nature and need of any special group, department, or division. What is truly needed is a flexible approach which can be adapted not only to different types of businesses, but also to the diversity of leaders and groups within any one business.

This lack of flexibility is probably the greatest single flaw in all the approaches used to date by the behavioral scientists. They seem to have a hard time understanding that if you are to have a universal theory which will lead to universal practice, you must have universal behavioral goals. The whole idea of universal goals of management behavior, goals to which all managers at all levels and in all functions will subscribe, is not only completely unrealistic but probably not at all desirable. It certainly defies the need for individual initiative and innovation.

The Need for Change

Talleyrand said, "The art of statesmanship is to foresee the inevitable and to expedite its occurrence." His unbelievably long and successful career under a succession of quite different sovereigns speaks well of his ability to accept the need for change. For most mortals, however, it is always difficult to rationalize a new way of thinking. It is particularly difficult if competition or other circumstances don't force the decision that *some* new way of thinking is required. It is not surprising, therefore, to find that top managers in many companies are not actively seeking new practices in the management development area. No decision is, quite yet, being forced for even some kind of change.

On the other hand, everybody will agree that things are not as they used to be. They never are and never were. People also are constantly changing, though not so rapidly. So, just as it pays the top manager to try to understand the trend of the way *things* are changing, it behooves him to try to understand the way people are changing. The ability to predict is the key to the ability to control in both instances.

The Management of Change

It takes only an ordinary administrator and a book of procedures to run something that doesn't change. The job of a manager, however, is to stay on top of change. The management, or control, of change is what management is meant to be all about. Sometimes the manager's job is to adapt to change; at other times it is to initiate change. The manager who resists change—who does not wholeheartedly agree with the concept of the need for, and desirability of, change—is basically an administrator.

Realistically, on the other hand, it must be recognized that those in authority often see a particular threat to their authority in any change in the ways of handling people. As with all innovations, this is felt most strongly when it takes place without their active participation and understanding. Top managers have a very human tendency to like best those changes in which they have played an active part, to the point where they can feel they themselves are the initiators.

The general working environment for managers is usually a direct reflection of their top executive. The kind of working environment to be found in any business organization will depend to a great extent on how the managers are managed. When viewed in this manner, most organizations divide themselves into three basic categories:

1. Those where most of the ideas tend to flow down from the top, usually accompanied by minimum freedom for initiative by others.

2. Those where emphasis is placed upon having the ideas flow upward through the organization and where top management spends more time listening than talking.

3. Those which haven't quite made up their minds and where there are many crosscurrents developed by individual managers selecting one or the other of the first two approaches.

One place where change is being forced is in larger corporations, where the sheer complexity of business problems is making it necessary to organize so that the maximum number of ideas can flow upward. The intentions are good and most companies in this category take pride in proclaiming that individual responsibility is firmly fixed at all levels of the organization and that emphasis is placed upon providing opportunities for all persons to realize their full potential. The role of the individual is accepted as greater than ever before. The recruiting literature emphasizes that the need was never greater for bright young minds and individuals of character to help make the organization run. The organization is looking for outstanding people who want quick responsibility and are capable of handling positions which are defined to a great extent by their own imaginations.

However, although the need is truly great, in practice the opportunities are often not quite as advertised because the control of managerial practices has not yet caught up with the preaching.

In the people-handling area there is prevalent among managers at all levels this weakness: They assume that subordinates are handling their people properly and continue to assume so until some cause célèbre occurs. This overconfidence seems to result from the natural tendency to see things as we want to see them and to see only what we are looking for. Every manager has plenty of problems already—he is not actively looking for another, particularly if it is in an area where he is not being pushed by his superiors and there is no solution immediately available. The management of change must, therefore, concentrate on opportunities to improve the effectiveness of the organization as a whole, not on discovering more problems that need solving.

It is also important to recognize that most managers who have received one or two promotions tend to consider themselves personnel experts, if not amateur psychologists. They have a pretty good idea of what the company is looking for: more people like themselves. They have learned by this time the buzz words that will turn their superiors on or off about one of their subordinates, and they outwardly demonstrate a feeling of personal security probably greater than they have any right to feel.

Not many managers in this group are going to admit to any need for outside help in handling their subordinate managers, or to readily accept it if offered. Their instincts tell them that this may constitute a real threat to their freedom of action and may very well end up developing into one more area where personal performance will be measured against specific objectives. In this connection, experience has indicated a tendency for resistance to be greatest among managers whose organizations actually do have very real problems. Fortunately, in most organizations these managers probably constitute a definite minority.

The approach to such individuals with real problems must be patterned to a certain extent after that used so successfully by Alcoholics Anonymous. The first, and most important, step is to get the person to recognize that he has a problem, and the second is to assure him that it is curable with effort. Most managers will not fall into this problem category and can become enthusiastic supporters of a program for change and improvement, particularly when the approach follows certain guidelines which experience has found to have the greatest chance of producing measurably successful results. These guidelines are summarized in Chapter 5.

Additional arguments in the rationale for change can be found in the emphasis of the past 20 years on higher education for more and more young people, which emphasis has been encouraged by most businesses. The general recognition of the growing needs of an increasingly technical and complex society has been reflected in the business community by the previously noted increase in the need for smart and able middle managers. If a big business is not to become a bureaucracy, it must avoid the typical bureaucratic organization which consists of a reasonably large number of smart and eager young people at the bottom and one or two very smart and able people at the top, with very little in the way of ability in between.

In the past few years most businesses have been increasingly pressured into paying greater attention to what particular groups of consumers (or their advocates) want, and to what local and national governments want. These new demands on the time and energies of the chief executive and other top managers have frequently distracted them from paying sufficient attention to the changing wants and needs of their own middle and lower management levels.

Some of these needs may not be considered reasonable, but they all need attention. Somebody must mind the store. A smart top management faced with these new and continuing distractions will either turn over responsibility for them to a newly created group of managers or, if it wants to remain personally involved to any large extent, will delegate down the line a greater share of the day-to-day operating responsibility. It is not likely, however, that any of these changes will automatically result in greater power or authority at the lower and middle levels.

In today's large business organizations the junior and middle managers have an increasing number of working relationships with managers in other departments or managers performing other functions, who are coequals, or peers. These working relationships tend to be on an ad hoc basis and can frequently result in an easy and candid rapport which is found to be stimulating because it is nonthreatening.

When such relationships are also found to be effective, there is a tendency, marked by many behavioral studies, for the participants to question the stricter linear relationships with decision makers up the line. This can then develop into an unreasonable resentment that unilateral authority has not been given to the peer group. The definitions of responsibility and authority and the relationship of the two have caused endless dissension and discussion, particularly among younger managers. but most of this is quite unnecessary, as we shall see later.

It has always seemed paradoxical that so many able individuals in top positions who justifiably pride themselves on their ability to "manage change" in research, marketing, or operations seem so reluctant to accept the need for managing change in the people sense. Perhaps the reason lies in the simple fact that top managers really don't like to make up their minds until they have to. It often takes outsiders a long time to appreciate that this is not a weakness, but a very practical approach which allows maximum flexibility. The missing ingredient in this instance may simply be that nobody has convinced top managers that they must take a position and involve themselves directly in this issue.

The business manager learns his particular business by constant observation and analysis of what is actually happening in order to understand cause and effect relationships. To assist him in this, a most elaborate and costly system for the processing of precise factual information has been developed over the last 20 or 30 years. A strong argument can be made that only with this same type of approach can any manager learn to understand and control the interpersonal relationships of managers within his particular organization. It is *his* particular business and *his* particular organization he must master, not all businesses or all organizations.

If the best, and perhaps only, way to understand anything fully is to experience it, it will be necessary for all levels of management to be involved directly in any analysis and development of plans for more effective management development within a specific group. Experience to date indicates that when the program is planned more or less exclusively by others in staff groups, or by outside consultants, the intended participants will tend to ignore it in actual operation through lack of interest or understanding.

The fact that a program to improve managerial behavior and effectiveness must involve all levels of management directly and continuously presents a major problem. This is because this kind of program must fully respect the time limitations of management, especially top management, as do all the other information systems designed to keep managers on top of the business. The approach discussed in the following chapters is designed to come to grips directly and practically with that problem.

Key Objectives of Management Development

Although much time and money have been spent on various types of organization and management development programs, most of these have lacked clearly stated objectives and the intent to measure results against these objectives. The following major objectives are recommended for any organization which decides to adopt a program to optimize the achievement level of its managers:

1. Provide a broader base of highly competent managers from which selection can be made for positions of highest responsibility.

2. Provide greater assurance that all managerial positions at all levels are filled with individuals competent to help in moving the business ahead.

3. Provide a working environment which ensures for each manager increased resources for his continuing growth and increased opportunities to use his powers and to achieve his full potential.

"Human Relations" Versus "Individual Relations"

The one thing which might help most to improve communications with regard to management development would be to ban the term "human relations." In the first place this suggests human nature, which all sorts of people are fond of saying never changes. It is easy to say that if human nature does not change, then ways of handling people do not need changing.

It can be further argued that the things which make us human are those which are common to all of us, whereas organizations exist essentially as a way of recognizing and emphasizing the things which make us different. And it is what makes us different—that is, our very individuality—that makes us difficult to deal with in an organizational framework.

Perhaps the term "individual relations" could be substituted for "human relations," since it emphasizes the need to treat people as individuals, as people different in some ways from us, and recognizes the all-important role that only the individual can play in an organization. When a sheep is acting most like a sheep, he is acting like all other sheep. It is the same with a human. The more he is thinking and acting like a human, the more he is thinking and acting like all other humans. This should be anathema at the managerial level, where it is usually only the imaginative, the different, the individual ideas and initiatives which, put into action, can keep the business moving ahead.

There is really no such entity as the X Corporation. What the corporation really *is* results entirely from what all its managers, acting as individuals, actually *do,* and the character of the corporation depends largely upon *how* they do it. These managers, at all levels, are continually interacting as individuals in the process of figuring out what needs to be done, deciding how to do it, and seeing that it gets done. When it comes to delivering a result, the manager is frequently acting, reacting, and interacting with other individuals who must be motivated to want the same objectives.

Such interactions involve a continuously changing combination of superiors, subordinates, and peers. These managers are sometimes closely associated in the same part of the organization but are frequently located in different line or staff areas or even in different organizations. Although formal coordination of levels or correlations of functions may be built into the organizational structure, the working relationships between managers naturally and properly tend to become quite individualized.

All organizations have policies, principles, and procedures which express their basic doctrines and disciplines, but these policies are meaningless without the disciples needed to carry them into action. The disciples are always individuals, each of whom consciously or unconsciously re-interprets the policies, principles, and procedures to a certain degree, because of his own personal habits and attitudes. The new attitudes and habits of each new crop of young management prospects tend to challenge established thinking and can cause serious gaps between presumed policy and actual practice.

In recent years, with the steady influx into management ranks of nonwhites, women, and other members of minority groups, challenges to established ways of thinking have increased in both number and variety. Many of these challenges are not easily resolved, but there is slowly developing an awareness that the key to effective control must lie in recognizing individual differences and accepting those that are not negative in their effect upon the organization as a whole.

The term most frequently associated with the large, modern corporation is "dynamic." This is not something thought up by a P.R. writer, and it does not carry automatic connotations of good or bad. It is, however, most descriptive. It refers to "forces not in equilibrium; pertaining to motion as the result of force; opposed to static."

It is not startling, therefore, to have the leaders of such organizations referred to most frequently as "dynamic businessmen." On the other hand, it *is* most unusual to hear reference to "dynamic managers" at the middle or lower levels. This may result from a tendency to think of top executives as individual leaders and most of the other managers as groups—the Plant Managers, the District Managers, the Product Managers, and so forth—almost as though they were only a system of cogs or replaceable parts rather than individual wheels.

All too frequently, it appears, managers at the middle and lower levels are considered as individuals only at the time they are hired, fired, or promoted. The rest of the time they are not considered as individuals, but as performers of specific functions or handlers of specific projects. Usually, only a manager's immediate superior will consistently recognize his individuality and only because close, daily contact makes this necessary. But, alas, the superior too frequently sees this individuality as a complicating factor which makes his control over operations more difficult.

It should be made clear that reference is not being made here to extraneous individual characteristics which should not be permitted to intrude upon the role which the subordinate must play, but to the basic individuality which is directly related to job performance.

the four r's
of performance 4

It takes far more science to understand human beings and their rights than to proclaim loudly our own rights and reasonableness.

Mary Parker Follett

The unreality of many management development concepts lies in their failure to recognize the need to relate properly the fundamentals of individual performance to those of organization performance. Largely because of this, the ideas have been difficult to put into practice, and, of course, only improved practices can lead to improved results. Experience indicates that the first step in any management development program must be to formulate the basic equations which do properly relate individuals and organization as they actually are.

In developing such equations it is necessary to determine and analyze the most fundamental sources of power and satisfaction for the individual and for the organization. There are many factors which enter any such equation, and these must be carefully culled with emphasis on maximum simplicity. The fundamentals are those factors which are inherent in all individual and organization performance and which most directly determine the level of results achievement. These basic factors can be grouped into four categories, which will be called the Four R's—*requisites, resources, responsibilities,* and *results.*

Next, within each of the four categories, the key pertinent factors should be analyzed. The factors are those which will have the greatest effect on achieving the best results and which can be factually measured. This can be done in separate steps for each of the four categories and the total then brought together in one equation.

It should be emphasized that the fundamentals of individual performance are essentially those of a manager in his subordinate position, while organization fundamentals are those of a manager or group of managers in the capacity of superior. All managers, except at the very bottom level, are continually operating in either a subordinate or superior capacity. These are the two faces which a manager must wear, and the equations relating the fundamentals will help him to wear these two faces without being two-faced.

It might further be added that the organization fundamentals constitute the basic system which each manager must master, rather than fight, to the point where he can make it work for him.

Maximizing Results

For the individual manager the results which it is desired to maximize consist of what he does to (1) move the business ahead, (2) develop others under him, and (3) advance himself. The results desired for the organization, which develop from the sum total of these individual results, are (1) profit, (2) growth, and (3) perpetuation. Maximizing individual results becomes the goal, because organization results automatically benefit and develop therefrom.

It must be recognized that how the organization (or group of superiors) looks at its required results has a lot to do with the kind of working environment in which the individual operates. There is usually a consistent pattern, and it is the individual's responsibility to understand this pattern and adapt himself accordingly. It will do him little good to recommend a short-term, highly opportunistic new venture to an organization interested only in carefully considered actions which give every indication of being profitable over a long period of time.

In the same area of profit interest, on the other hand, the observant individual whose antennae tell him that the organization is expecting to enjoy a particularly good year based upon the first six months' results and future forecasts, may find a particularly opportune time to recommend a capital expenditure.

Understanding the way the organization perpetuates itself is equally important to the individual. If above everything else he wants to be president and in a position to tell everybody else how to run the business by no later than age 35, he would usually be ill advised to look for this opportunity in a large corporation. Again, if the organization is one where most of the middle managers are relative old-timers and where top executives are for the most part brought in from the outside, it says something about the general caliber of management and opportunities for personal growth.

On the other hand, if the organization has a successful record and takes pride in developing all its management from within, there is a fair degree of assurance that everyone in a key position is a known quantity with proven ability to work well with others in the organization, who have also grown up with it.

For the younger manager in this kind of organization, there is a form of guarantee that a good try will be made to prepare him or her for increasing responsibilities, since the future growth and perpetuation of the organization can come only from building the strength of younger management. A high rate of turnover can be expected in the lower ranks and a relatively low rate in the higher ranks of management—the opposite of what generally occurs in the company which does not develop its own top management from within.

The successful business will show a certain consistency in the pattern of profits and growth, and in the way it goes about perpetuating itself. In similar fashion the successful manager will demonstrate consistency in moving the business ahead, developing others, and self-advancement. These results of both the organization and the individual are factual and measurable and are not easily subject to misinterpretation.

Of course, moving the business ahead may involve a different kind of result in manufacturing (increased productivity from a unit) than in sales (a new and more effective approach to a particular type of customer) or in research (a better and yet more economical product formulation or process). The development of other managers may be a more important result for a manager in a higher-level position or in a large marketing department than in a small plant engineer's office. In different parts of the business there may be differences in degree of opportunity for self-advancement "up the ladder," but all managers, wherever they are, should have an equal commitment to self-advancement in terms of continually learning to become better managers.

Minimizing Conflicts in Responsibility

The preceding definition of "results" has been very deliberately designed to avoid the confusion which so frequently occurs between performance of responsibilities and achievement of results. The expression is often heard that a certain manager "gets results," but this means different things to different people. It may mean a subordinate finally did something his superior wanted done, that the subordinate is good at seeing that things get done, or that he simply achieved a specific assigned objective. There is nothing wrong with these accomplishments, but they should not form the sole basis of a reputation for getting results. It might be well to point out that the manager who understands the kind of results wanted by his superiors is way ahead of the one who doesn't—which is the reason for defining the category with considerable care.

A case in point is provided from the author's younger days, by his experiences with two superiors. Under the first, the subordinate obtained results which moved the business ahead and developed others but didn't advance himself, because the results were not considered important by his superior. That executive was the type who kept to himself his ideas on the results he wanted, and nobody ever seemed to measure up to his expectations, so that his record for developing other managers was miserable.

The subordinate was later transferred to another location and there was able to get the top manager to discuss what the latter thought was most needed at that location. The superior had about ten things on his mind, and immediately after the talk, the subordinate wrote them down so that they would not be forgotten. Then, within the next year, he accomplished all of them, one by one. Needless to say, he received a very large promotion in responsibilities shortly thereafer.

Still on the subject of confusion between performance of responsibilities and achievement of results, it is quite possible for an individual to seem to perform his responsibilities without making any significant contributions in terms of moving the business ahead or developing others. Such an individual is really more of an administrator than a manager. "Results" should be defined only as *what happened*, not how it happened. "Performance" will then be considered the manner in which responsibilities are performed to achieve results. It is important that the individual and the organization be evaluated on the basis of both accomplishment of erd results and performance of responsibilities.

Since we are anticipating the possibility of conflict between the responsibilities of the individual and those of the organization, it will help to look first at those responsibilities of the organization (a group of superiors) which are most essential to its survival. They are *leadership, authority,* and *controls.* Just mentioning those words suggests the danger of conflict with the individual, whose fundamental responsibilities are *initiating, influ-*

encing, and *administering* his part of the operations.

Organization leadership should be primarily concerned with the establishment of goals, the determination of priorities, and the allocation of resources. In most modern organizations this is not something which can be done by any one individual at the top all by himself. To a great extent the goals, priorities, and allocations of resources develop from ideas to move the business ahead, which are initiated by a large number of individual managers down the line.

The good executive who understands organization leadership is, therefore, conscious of the need to encourage new ideas from his subordinates. He does not see his responsibility in terms of dominating the thinking of subordinates. He sees it, rather, in terms of selecting from an up-the-line flow of practicable ideas those combinations of ideas which come closest to meeting his goals within available resources. In the same way, his options and priorities become established not so much by what he personally would like to do, but by what he can do and must do with plans developed mostly by others.

Leadership is frequently thought of in terms of personal abilities and described in terms which make it a subjective quality. Traditionally, an aggressive personality has been considered a key indicator of individual leadership. In sales, for example, the dominating individual who could make the customer do what he, the salesman, wanted was frequently the model. Today, with salesmen and customer often on more equal ground, there is much less emphasis on dominating the customer and much more on understanding him as an individual, what his needs are, and how he can make the best use of the salesman's products.

In this present situation, the salesman is still exerting leadership and control, but much more through his grasp *of* the situation rather than by his grasp *on* the other person. And the most important thing which grows out of this grasp of the situation is what initiatives the salesman takes.

Authority and controls are very directly related to organization leadership. "Authority" and "discipline" are practically synonymous terms in this context. Essential as they are to the organization, they at the same time constitute a continuing potential threat to the freedom of thinking required for the exercise of individual initiative.

Authority is associated directly with position, and also with function and with the situation. A large body of evidence indicates that by minimizing the authority of position and permitting the authority of function and situation to control the decision-making process, the effectiveness of a total management group can be expected to improve.

Any manager-leader who is more interested in achieving results than in exercising the rights of his position will always be seeking ways to encourage his subordinates to share in the decision-making process. He will also place emphasis on the proper use of controls to help determine when it is necessary to intervene and to exert the leadership and authority of his superior position.

Organization controls should exist primarily to provide essential information which can be continually evaluated so as to tell the superior when his intervention is needed. This should be true not just for leaders at the top, but for all superior managers in dealing with subordinates. Intervention is a positive corollary of delegation. The propriety of each intervention will depend largely upon the demands of available time, the relative importance of the project, and its newness to the managers involved. No good manager at any level who is faced with a unique situation of critical importance to the organization is going to resent constructive intervention by any number of superiors. He may quite rightfully resent similar intervention in more ordinary circumstances.

Looked at in this way, the superior manager, when providing the leadership, authority, and control essential to the organization as a whole, must be interested in exerting these so as to allow the greatest possible freedom for subordinate managers to perform their basic responsibilities.

Any subordinate manager will tell you it can be really tough to work directly for a superior who was just promoted from the position the subordinate now holds. It can also be rewarding—if the superior is smart enough not to let his parallel thinking show through too clearly and lets go of the primary responsibility. Certainly, it is much more difficult to work for or try to communicate clearly with a superior who doesn't know much, if anything, about your operations.

A good friend who was V.P., marketing, in another company was once asked to make an important 20-minute advertising budget presentation to the board of directors. He felt confident because he knew that recent advertising expenditures had been directly related to a great improvement in volume and market share for the product involved.

Trained to think in terms of trusting the tried and force-feeding the success, he had built a strong case for heavier expenditures based upon the healthy trends.

However, before he could even begin his presentation, the chairman of the board, who had come up through the financial end of the business, said he would like to ask one preliminary question. To the V.P.'s consternation, the question was "Why, if the business is so healthy, is it necessary to spend all the money currently being spent on advertising?"

Just as the organization responsibilities are those most directly related to results, the individual responsibilities of *initiating, influencing,* and *administering* are directly related to the desired individual results. These are fundamental factors which can be factually measured and attributed to an individual. One of the biggest problems which sometimes arises in the evaluation of managers is the difficulty of determining just which individual is to receive the main credit for results obtained by a group effort. However, a good case can be made for crediting the individual who initiated the action.

As used in this discussion, the term "initiating" does not refer to "initiative," the noun, which is often used in subjective evaluations and suggests self-starting ability. Instead, it refers to "initiate," the verb, which describes what the manager actually *does* in terms of how he thinks, decides, and acts. Initiating involves assessing where his particular operation is now and planning where he wants it to be and how he is going to get it there. To initiate means to develop good, practicable ideas which will move the business ahead.

It can fairly be said that in any particular organization there will be a high percentage of managers who are pretty good at getting things done, a reasonable percentage who are imaginative in figuring out how something should be done, and a relatively small percentage who are really good at planning, or figuring out what needs to be done in the first place.

Many managers, particularly younger managers in large organizations, could considerably improve their ability to plan by appreciating and tapping the tremendous resources available to them in the form of other good minds and the experience of others. To initiate also includes making the necessary decisions and taking the necessary action. It usually grows out of the manager's complete sense of responsibility for the area entrusted to him, not only for his own work but for the work of others which will affect his.

In the process of initiating a good, practicable idea, the individual quickly appreciates his second basic responsibility, which is influencing. Here again, use of the noun "influence" is not intended. The noun is usually something which through personality or position becomes a quality, with some of the attributes of a club or long leverage stick. "Influence," the verb, describes an action, what the manager actually *does* in making his thinking felt up and down the organization. It applies to how well he understands the needs of the business and other individuals, adapts to those needs, and also succeeds in making his own thinking understood in a way that influences the thinking of the organization. If the idea he proposes is a new one, it will not be familiar to others and the job of influencing may be tough. Influencing involves *communication, coordination,* and *cooperation.*

Communication has been defined as the ability to express oneself precisely, concisely, and to the point, both orally and in writing. But effective communications, the *act* of communicating, requires making oneself understood and understanding others, listening as well as talking, and selling others on one's idea or a reasonable facsimile thereof. Businessmen did this orally for centuries before they learned to read and write. But today, particularly in large corporations, the talking time of top managers is at a premium, and communication with them must be principally in writing.

A real dedication to mastering this most essential of managerial skills is required for any individual who wants to progress very far. It demands only observation and determination, plus, occasionally, a sense of humor. Some superiors, for example, develop a fetish about certain words. An important recommendation may be held up so that the word "discontinuation" can be changed to "discontinuance." Later, another superior may toss back a recommendation because he doesn't care for the word "discontinuance." Other superiors may suffer severe labor pains when confronted with "conceive" or "conception." There is really nothing wrong with this, particularly if it serves to teach the writer to keep in mind the person to whom he is addressing his message.

Coordination of the various levels and functions involved in putting any idea into action frequently involves delegation. Delegation requires not only a clear understanding of the goals and objectives but a knowledge of, and appreciation for, the diverse abilities of others. Effective delegation usually entails a certain amount of freedom for the subordinate to use his personal initiative in deciding how the job is to be done and taking action to see that it gets done. This kind of delegation is not easy for the superior to perform, particularly if the job is not a simple one, unless he has real confidence in the subordinate and the goals and objectives are completely clear.

What is being discussed here is, of course, not the delegation which is automatically structured into the organization chart, but the day-to-day delegation which takes place on a less formalized basis. One good rule, which has many times been proved in practice, is this: When some particularly important project is to be implemented with dispatch or with unusual thoroughness, it is wise to give one individual overall responsibility. This does not mean he has unilateral authority; it does mean that he will be held uniquely accountable for results, including the work of all those involved over whom he explicitly does not have direct authority. In such cases the necessary authority tends to grow out of the situation.

The kind of assignment referred to above constitutes a good test of a manager's ability to secure cooperation, one of the three essential elements in influencing. The relative newcomer to management ranks may, at first, be surprised by the difficulty he encounters in securing the cooperation of others. He lacks sufficient exposure to other levels and functions to appreciate that a consensus on the ultimate goal can coexist with much disagreement on the specific objectives which will serve to achieve it.

Within the different departmental areas and supervisory levels there are always many points of view on the more specific goals and objectives needed to achieve these major end results. When such crosscurrents are particularly strong, cooperation is not always easily obtained. Similarly, cooperation is sometimes achieved with surprising ease, because it happens to coincide with something entirely separate which is desired by the cooperating individual.

The third basic responsibility of the manager is administering, or seeing that things get done. This should be the easiest part of the job, but it is not always so, because any good manager always has more than he can readily handle and each day tends to bring new crises. The ability to operate under pressure, to react intelligently to ever-changing pressures and priorities, and to persevere until the job is done is, once again, a very individual matter. The major problem, particularly for the younger and less experienced manager, is to handle the job of administering in such a way that he has the time for the even more important jobs of initiating and influencing.

In minimizing conflicts between individual and organization responsibilities, the superior manager should tend to give the benefit of any doubt to the subordinate manager. The superior, representing the leadership, authority, and control responsibilities of the organization, must realize the extent to which their careful exercise can maximize the successful performance of individual responsibilities. Above all, he must try to avoid assuming the individual's responsibility for initiating in the mistaken impression that he is thereby demonstrating his own leadership.

Improving and Enlarging Resources

The resources of the manager and the organization might be viewed as the basic sources of power for the exercise of responsibilities and the achievement of results. Of the many skills and abilities that fall into this category, the most important are those resources which are directly related to responsibilities and results and which can be expanded and improved. They *must*, in fact, be expanded and improved if the individual is to handle increasing responsibilities, or even do a better job of handling current responsibilities. Viewed in this light, the most fundamental resources of the effective manager are *knowledge, imagination,* and *reason:* a knowledge of the job, of the business, and of people; an imagination which promotes creative thinking in terms of what is, what can be, and what should be; and an ability to reason which can analyze, synthesize, and organize facts and ideas.

The basic resources of the organization are *procedures, policies,* and *principles.* These have been developed out of experience, and when kept up to date and representative of what experience says works best, they can be of invaluable service to the manager who learns to master the system—something which all good managers must do. To a great extent these resources of the organization are directly related to, and frequently grow out of, the basic resources of the individual manager.

The primary purposes of procedures should be to assist in the coordination of levels of management, in the correlation of the different functions of management, and in the simplification of communications between different parts of the organization. A procedure is frequently a considerably detailed step-by-step guideline for handling a specific action which is frequently repeated. In fact, it has generally been found desirable to limit procedures as much as possible to those actions which recur often, so as to simplify the actions and avoid repeating mistakes. Procedures are, for the most part, "how to" instruments. Overemphasis on procedure is what leads to bureaucracy.

Policies are more important than procedures and to a greater extent reflect the careful thinking of top management on who is responsible, what the responsibilities are, and how they are to be carried out. In well-managed organizations, the more important policies are almost always in writing and are made available on a need-to-know basis to those responsible to see that practice follows policy. Policies reflect the basic character of the organization, indicating not only what is to be done by whom, but in many instances how various managers are supposed to interrelate.

Principles of the organization are usually basic ways of thinking. To the extent that they are improved, enlarged and collected, and analyzed and evaluated for what works best, the principles of the organization tend to reflect what experience has shown to be most efficient and effective. Experience, which is constantly changing, cannot be expected to be transmitted entirely through organizational procedures, policies, and principles. It is, therefore, most important that centers be established for the collection, analysis, and evaluation of data relating to what works best, and that meaningful ways be found to impart to individual managers the broader experience being gained by the organization as a whole. It is, of course, the responsibility of each manager to learn, to understand, and to master the system, but principles, since they are frequently not in writing, can be subject to much personal interpretation.

The leaders of any organization should always be seeking ways in which the basic resources of each manager can be enlarged and improved in their application to his job. This means careful attention to positioning the individual not only where he has opportunity to gain personal experience, but where he can also learn the maximum from the experience of others who have related responsibilities. By being exposed to what seems to work best, and not to work, for these other managers, he can augment his own resources.

What is being suggested here is not some new system for "teaching" what seems to have been learned by others. It is, rather, a program of exposing a manager to the actual mistakes and successes of others in a way that permits him to learn for himself as he draws his own conclusions and acquires a broader understanding. This kind of learning exercise can never be criticized as spoon-feeding since it is not telling someone how to think but simply broadening his base of experience against which to think. It would be a safe guess that very few companies have made even a bare beginning in this most important area. However, such efforts are essential if the resources of the individual manager and the organization are to be improved and enlarged.

Harmonizing Requisites

The requisites we are seeking are fundamental factors which can be measured and controlled, and which would appear to have the most significant influence on achievement level. Therefore, the individual requisites would seem to be *money, status,* and *opportunity,* not necessarily in that order, and those of the organization to be *hiring, firing,* and *retaining.*

Taking the organization's requisites first, it is surprising how much more frequently reference is made to hiring and firing than to the equally important factor of holding, or retaining, good managers. Maybe this is because so many managers are fishermen who most enjoy catching the elusive and throwing back those that are not keepers, without taking as much interest in the food value of those already in the creel.

In any event, the retention of good managers is important to the efficiency and effectiveness of operations. In a nutshell it involves paying them right, handling them right, and putting them in the right job. This sometimes includes making sure they are working for the right kind of person, since personality conflicts do, and always will, exist. It is hard to do all this without some kind of planned development program which relates the organization's requisites to the individual's requisites of money, status, and opportunity.

The same is true of hiring practices. Good hiring practices will similarly recognize these individual requisites, whether the employee sought is a college recruit or a vice-president from another firm. Good hiring practices involve searching in the right places, selecting with care, and then making sure to secure those selected.

"Firing" is an unpleasant word which is sometimes changed to something more pleasant like "involuntary termination" or "mutual agreement that future prospects look brighter elsewhere." It is something which must be done on a continuing basis by any organization, however. Sometimes it is a simple matter of the individual's money or status goals outstripping the organization's best estimate of where he might end up if he remained. At other times it can be the individual's inability to take advantage of opportunities to learn, develop, and apply. A voluntary termination in which the manager unilaterally decides to leave almost always involves one or more of the requisites money, status, and opportunity.

There can be little doubt that it will pay any manager to know intimately the specific requisites of each subordinate manager reporting directly to him. These tend to include very personal attitudes and needs which vary greatly among individuals and also within any one individual as he progresses in the ranks of management. Sensitivity, imagination, and factual knowledge of the other person are frequently needed to keep these requisites from becoming negatives and to harmonize them in a way which will encourage the natural self-starting ability of the subordinate.

In the area of money, one of the best examples of imaginative thinking the author ever experienced was employed by the head of a small fast-growing company. In need of several able young managers with three to five years' experience in business, he estimated that it would cost him several thousand dollars apiece to secure such managers through a search firm. Therefore, he simply approached several prospects employed by a large company noted for its careful selection and training of young managers.

His first question to the young executive was how much money did he have in the bank, knowing it probably was near zero. His second question was how would he like to have several thousand dollars in the bank tomorrow morning. With the addition of a few nice words about status and opportunity, his ratio of success in securing a number of very capable managers was, not surprisingly, close to 100 percent. Despite this imaginative ploy, however, his success ratio would undoubtedly have been much lower if certain superiors of the larger company had applied some of the same imagination to the opportunity, status, and money needs of those subordinates who were enticed away.

Obviously, no superior can always treat a subordinate as he would like to be treated, but nobody expects that.

A deliberate effort to create a special opportunity for the subordinate, a request for and acceptance of his judgment on a relatively simple matter, or an expression of "well done" for a particular job will go a long way, as can a little creative thinking in the timing of a salary increase, just every now and then. A well-timed, unexpected salary increase often provides a longer-lasting stimulant than an expected one. Status is too frequently associated with position, although it basically involves the individual's feeling that he is needed, heeded, and appreciated, which is something quite different.

Advantages of This System

There are several important advantages in this system of equating the fundamentals (the Four R's) of the individual manager with those of the organization:

1. The system can apply to managers at all levels and to any part of any organization or to the organization as a whole, with differences only in degree of emphasis given to any particular fundamental.

2. The system is flexible, so that it is possible to select for attention and improvement any specific fundamental of the individual or the organization; or any group of fundamentals, such as resources; or, over a period of time, all four groups (requisites, resources, responsibilities, and results). It is thus possible to focus attention immediately on those areas where the leader of a particular group and his immediate subordinates agree there is the greatest opportunity for improvement, or the greatest positive gain to be obtained by improvement.

3. The system relates the fundamentals of individual and organization in a way which makes both the beneficiaries of any change for the better.

In any sport or other form of competitive activity there are always certain fundamentals that can be ignored only at your peril. In the final analysis, good management might be likened to the good golf swing, where the desired result is to strike the ball squarely. There are many different ways to achieve this result, and each golfer's methods depend somewhat on his particular mental and physical endowments.

However, the good golfer is a student of the game and knows that there are certain fundamentals of grip, stance, backswing, and downswing which are common to all good golfers. The individual can make minor modifications in these to suit personal needs, but his game is sure to deteriorate rapidly if he ignores any of the fundamentals. The trouble with too many management development programs is that they are based on one individual's theory about how the game should be played, rather than on analysis of the fundamentals common to all good performers.

Any program to raise the level of achievement in a larger percentage of managers—when it is based on, and limited to, the fundamentals—will help all managers and can in no way hurt the game of the naturally endowed top performer. This refutes the common argument that management development programs tend to become a crutch for the weak which makes it more difficult to identify the best.

What is being suggested is that the approach to management development be similar to that used so successfully in many other areas of business, but seldom, if ever, applied to the people end of a business. For example, there is a concept of forward planning known as total marketing, which is accepted by successful consumer products companies. This is designed to obtain the broadest possible level of initial trial and repurchase for a product. The product is developed to provide maximum consumer satisfaction and marketability, packaged to provide optimum in-store shelf impact and in-home consumer appeal, and marketed with strong and continuing advertising and sales promotion support.

When all of these things are right for a specific product, and keyed to each other, you have what is called a total marketing plan, which should produce the long-term brand loyalty that, in turn, builds a solid consumer franchise. This entire total marketing concept grows out of a knowledge of the consumer and the particular consumer-product relationship which permits the wants and needs of the consumer and of the producer to be mutually satisfied. The approach is based on the premise that if something is knowable, it's a sin not to know it and that fact is preferred to opinion.

What should be sought in any program to improve managerial performance is a similar total plan based upon greater knowledge of each manager and the peculiar individual-organization relationship which permits the wants and needs of both to be mutually satisfied in a way which produces better results. The superiority of fact to opinion is just as relevant here as it is in all other aspects of the business.

This type of approach permits the top manager to be tuned in on his organization in a way which enables him to anticipate and to lead. It's a bit like bird shooting, where you miss if you don't lead, but miss just as much if you lead too little or too much, and familiarity with a particular bird's flight pattern is the key to connecting

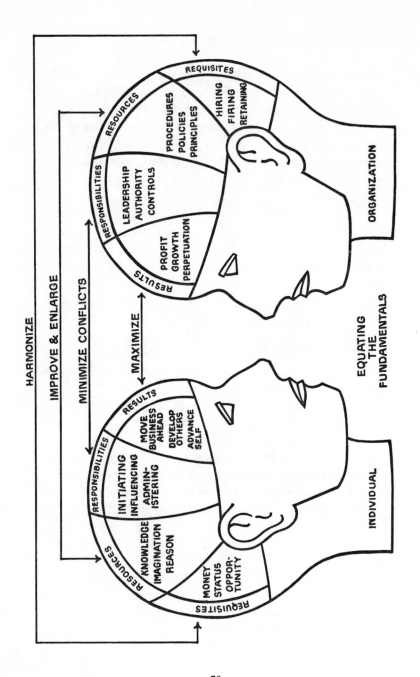

HARMONIZE

IMPROVE & ENLARGE

MINIMIZE CONFLICTS

MAXIMIZE

ORGANIZATION

REQUISITES

RESOURCES

HIRING
FIRING
RETAINING

PROCEDURES
POLICIES
PRINCIPLES

RESPONSIBILITIES

LEADERSHIP
AUTHORITY
CONTROLS

PROFIT
GROWTH
PERPETUATION

RESULTS

INDIVIDUAL

RESULTS

MOVE
BUSINESS
AHEAD

DEVELOP
OTHERS

ADVANCE
SELF

RESPONSIBILITIES

INITIATING
INFLUENCING

ADMIN-
ISTERING

RESOURCES

KNOWLEDGE
IMAGINATION
REASON

MONEY
STATUS
OPPOR-
TUNITY

REQUISITES

EQUATING
THE
FUNDAMENTALS

70

consistently. All managers are made up of different combinations of strengths and weaknesses. The primary objective in a program for improvement is to discover what works best and to maximize this throughout the organization. In the process, each individual must learn, over a period of time, how to maximize his strengths and control his weaknesses so that they don't get in the way of his strengths.

To serve as an easy reminder, the equation of the Four R's is briefly summarized in the chart on the facing page. It should be borne in mind that the exact terminology used is less important than the relationships between the fundamentals of the individual and those of the organization. Most important to remember is the need for factual measurement of the various factors for proper evaluation and control.

custom-tailoring your development program

5

We are more easily persuaded, in general, by the reasons we ourselves discover than by those which are given to us by others.

Blaise Pascal

Promoting the Best Practices

The practices to be sought for both the individual manager and the organization are those that help most to maximize their results, enlarge and increase their resources, minimize their conflicts in responsibility, and harmonize their requisites. (See the chart at the end of the last chapter.) After these best practices have been discovered or, as may frequently be found necessary, further developed, the next step is to promote them throughout the organization. Change is inevitable, but change does not inevitably lead to progress and improvement, so it is the management of *desired* change with which your management development program must be concerned.

It was noted earlier that managers as individuals have two separate and distinct sets of abilities in varying degrees and combinations—those abilities related to advancing themselves and those abilities related to advancing the business. Similarly, they engage in two separate and distinct types of practices—those actions which are taken to advance the business, and those activities primarily concerned with the individual's relations with other managers above, below, and at the same level.

There appears to be a definite correlation between the abilities required to advance the self and the practices involving relations with others. There is, of course, also a correlation between the abilities and the practices which relate to advancing the business.

There is a tremendous variation in abilities and practices not only among managers as a whole but also within any manager at different stages in his career. The recruit just out of college may need a couple of years to learn enough about the business to be in a position to make a real contribution toward advancing it; an experienced manager can move from one responsibility to another and make a significant contribution in the first month. On the other hand, the recruit may have abilities approaching the genius level in advancing himself, while the experienced manager may be a slow learner in this area.

In any management development program seeking out the practices that work best, it is necessary to uncover specific actions which have resulted in advancing the business and also those practices involved in the interaction of the individual and the organization. Examples of the first type might be the writing of buying specifications for cans which results in greatly improved machine efficiencies in the factory, a new sales promotion idea with higher consumer appeal, a new idea for advertising copy which results in increased sales, a product improvement or package change which does the same.

In a very small company it is possible that others will automatically learn about these actions and check them out for possible broader application. In the large corporation and particularly the multinational company, special methods need to be established so that successful practices in one area will be known by other areas.

There is a wealth of experience concerning what works and doesn't work which can be developed into a tremendously valuable resource. Examples of practices involving interactions of the individual manager and the organization include such matters as the creative use of a salary increase, improved interviewing techniques, handling of grievances on the factory floor, the conduct of a performance review with a subordinate, and all the other practices involved in harmonizing the requisites, enlarging and improving the resources, minimizing conflicts in responsibility, and maximizing results.

Maintaining Flexibility

The chart equating individual and organizational requisites, resources, responsibilities, and results emphasizes the extent to which changes in practices can be designed to benefit both the individual and the organization. The chart also serves to establish the parameters for a management development program as follows: It limits the number of basic factors involved in better performance results and relates those factors to each other in a way which permits any top manager to select for attention at any time those areas of operations which seem to be most promising in terms of potential improvement.

There is, therefore, a great deal of flexibility built into this way of thinking about management development. The leader of any particular part of a total organization can select what *he* wants and needs for *his* particular operation. These wants and needs of top managers will be found to vary considerably by department or division, such as manufacturing, sales, research, and the like. However, the basic factors in the chart hold true generally for all parts of the organization and for all levels of management. It is only their relative importance and relationship to each other which changes with different parts of the organization. This flexibility must be considered essential to any reality-oriented program which expects to produce measurable results.

There is no need to adhere rigidly to any system of rules, and the program can vary in keeping with the style of leadership in any particular part of the organization. The equation of fundamental requirements helps to assure a reasonably conservative approach which minimizes risks. It will be found that adherence to these fundamentals will almost automatically lead to sound thinking and the kind of tough-minded approach which can make a good idea a better idea or prove a seemingly good idea to be not so good after all.

Guidelines for Change and Improvement

By their nature, programs involving managerial behavior carry the risk of obtaining unanticipated and unwanted results. Such results can, at the least, waste time and, at the worst, cause a negative attitude toward further efforts for change and improvement. A considerable body of experience indicates that certain guidelines can be applied to a management development program which will do much to avoid those unwanted results. Used intelligently, in conjunction with the equation of fundamentals, these guidelines need in no way limit the flexibility of the program. The guidelines are listed below:

1. A management development program should be developed by the top manager and his immediate subordinates to accomplish what they specifically want for their organization. Effective effort can be defined as the putting of good experience into action. It is therefore most important to recognize that where this experience exists and how it can best be utilized in a particular part of any organization is usually best known by the top manager and his immediate subordinates. Their selection of areas for emphasis can be based on this knowledge. Any productive interpretation of the chart of fundamentals eventually requires the perceptions of not just one manager, but of all the managers who are interacting with one another at all levels.

These different individual perceptions must be brought out into the open where they can be observed by all. Discussion will be productive in direct ratio to the extent to which individual managers are willing and able to communicate their ideas and feelings, based upon their perceptions of what is actually happening, and the extent to which they can understand and respond to others in the group. The altered perceptions which result will then provide the basis for change and improvement in actual practice.

The purpose, of course, is not to get everybody thinking alike, but thinking in a disciplined way against a particular set of factors with a better appreciation of the different perceptions of others. Similarly, the object of this activity is not so much to make problems disappear as to learn better through shared experience how to cope with problems and to keep them from interfering with higher levels of individual and organizational achievement.

2. Nothing in this approach should be interpreted as suggesting group rule or committee decision in deciding what practices should be analyzed or how they might be changed. Decisions, when needed, should be made by the top manager of the group, and he must be permitted to veto opening up particularly sensitive areas. To be arbitrary on occasion must remain the inalienable right of the top manager in any program properly oriented to reality. However, the good manager will use this right as infrequently as he can.

In other words, the true needs of the organization must be given precedence when absolutely necessary over the needs of the individual manager. The important phrase is "when absolutely necessary," and it will be found that a well-conducted program will tend to reduce the frequency of such occasions.

3. An evolutionary, rather than revolutionary, approach has been found to be preferable. Areas for immediate and longer-term attention should be selected from the chart of fundamentals so as to maximize the chances of success early in the program. In this way it will be found that the program can become an integral part of the management process on a continuing, long-term basis.

4. One of the first steps should be to establish a thorough understanding of the ways in which current policies and practices tend to equate the fundamental

requirements of the individual and the organization. Since the purpose of a development program is to bring these more in line with each other, any current policy or procedure which cannot reasonably be expected to be followed in normal practice should be discarded.

5. Specific objectives should be clearly defined and the ways in which actual results will be measured against these objectives should be determined. Since the purpose of the entire program is to find practices which really bring about improvement, methods for factual measurement are as important as the objectives themselves. Where the results of an objective would not permit factual measurement, such an objective should be discarded in favor of one where proper measurement is feasible.

6. Finally, it should be recognized that any program, even one with limited initial objectives, will demand that time and effort be carved out of an already busy day, on a regular and continuing basis, until the program becomes a habit. It is the practice and not the preaching that pays off. The creation of new habits of practice requires that each manager become more constructively critical of his own practices. It has been found that a manager can be most constructively critical of his efforts when he shares with his superiors a basic understanding of his responsibility—and also shares in establishing goals. Although a particular job has been built into the structure of the organization, it should still be defined by the individual who performs it, and no two managers are ever going to define their job in exactly the same way.

All of this points once again to the need for the top manager to find the time to stay close to the program on a continuing basis in order to make sure that individual interpretations do not cause parts of his organization to stray off on undesirable and time-wasting tangents.

Definition of Measurable Goals

The basic equation of individual and organization fundamentals emphasizes that the results, or what might be called the final goals, of the manager are compatible with, and in many instances essential to, the desired results, or goals, of the organization. In a similar way the minimizing of conflicts in responsibilities, the improvement and enlargement of resources, and the harmonizing of requisites become goals which can be accepted as challenging and worthwhile by all concerned.

Rather than trying to *measure* subjective variables such as attitude, motivation, or morale, attention is thus focused on factors which can be more objectively measured and which will *result* in good attitudes, good motivation, and good morale. A program following this approach can, therefore, be presented to all concerned in a way that makes clear that its purpose is not to add more problems to the operations but to obtain more effective results by enlarging the resources and improving the performance of individual managers.

In this connection, it will usually be found that the way a manager perceives things and feels about a particular situation is the result of the manner in which he is oriented to his superiors, subordinates, and peers. The mature manager is well oriented to all three, and any program should be designed to assist in this orientation by increasing his exposure to superior levels.

There has always been a considerable amount of talk about "know-how" in management circles. Heard less often, but more important to the success of most organizations, is "know-what." Knowing what you want to do and what is needed comes before the know-how and actual doing. Also, unless what is wanted has been clearly defined and understood in terms of goals and objectives, there is, of course, no sure way of knowing when you have achieved a desired result. The secret of success for any program to increase individual achievement levels lies in knowing what is wanted and then using the entire organization's know-how to get it. As somebody once said of power, "If it's worth having, it's worth pursuing."

In initiating a program by deciding which areas are to be given attention at a particular point in time, notice must be taken of those areas where knowledge of current practices is probably limited. It must be remembered that the purpose is to seek not what should be happening ideally, but what is happening that works particularly well. It can be automatically assumed that actual practices will differ to a considerable degree because of the basic individuality of each manager, which should be preserved. The most important thing becomes the degree by which any one manager's practices differ from those of others and the extent to which this is conducive, or detrimental, to his and the organization's performance.

It is the recognition of individual differences, and their acceptance when not detrimental, which permits each manager to learn from others in a nonthreatening way. Together they permit him to define his job with his own imagination and to establish his own even higher standards, with a fuller appreciation of what he can and cannot do.

Sharing Successful Experience

There appears to be a natural tendency for people to exaggerate what they have learned from personal experience. Perhaps this is because they have found it difficult to learn constructively from the experience of others. It is doubtful that there is any basic mental block against learning from others, so their difficulty in learning must result from the manner in which that experience has either been hidden or predigested in attempts to "teach them." We do know that the body rejects direct transplants of most organs, except for brief periods of time. The mind also seems incapable of accepting any direct transplant of insight or judgment from another. Even two individuals who share an experience will gain different things from it, and part of the gain may come from observing the different reactions of the other.

Sharing experience in terms of what works best is an essential ingredient in the suggested approach to a program of improvement. It is comforting, therefore, to note that anthropologists have stated that shared experience seems to be built into the very nature of man. They add that it tends to be most evident when survival is at stake.

Business managers have noted that shared experience is also particularly evident when the goal is an unusually ambitious or exciting one so that there is "plenty of room for everybody to be a hero" or all can feel they are a part of something bigger and more important than themselves. The more astute business managers have also learned from history that ambition and suspicion seem to go hand in hand and that the higher the ambitious man rises, the more he is suspicious of others around him.

It might be well to recognize that the idea of sharing experience does not come easily to the most ambitious managers, so that it is essential to establish clearly the kind of successful experience which is going to be shared.

There is a danger that the idea of sharing successful experience might be viewed in the same light as so many theories of participative management, which one observant critic has said usually end up with everybody participating and the same few continuing to manage. The *purpose* is not participation. The *need* is for participation, because that is the only way to get the necessary input. The *need* is for participation, because that is the only way in which the individual and the organization can exist for their mutual benefit, rather than their mutual exploitation. The *need* is for participation, because that is the only way to get at what is actually happening and to build the necessary—but sadly lacking—history of successful experience in management practices.

In order to develop a history of successful experience, it will be found most useful to concentrate upon objective descriptions of what is, and is not, happening as a result of what managers actually do, and don't do. What must be avoided is qualitative judgments of what managers should be doing based on assumptions of capability, or subjective descriptions of what they think they do.

The most practical way for a manager to provide objective descriptions is with some form of written record. This will also be of great value in later evaluations of individual performance and corrective action. Here again we can see the importance of the basic chart. Maintaining a running diary of what is happening, like maintaining any personal diary, presents a major problem: What is to be put into it? The equation chart serves as a basis for selecting agreed areas for concentrated attention. Once this agreement is reached, the pertinent facts regarding what a manager does in this area are recorded, as are any results of his actions which appear to be good.

In order to avoid a mass of detailed evidence which is difficult both to collect and to make available to other managers in a meaningful form, agreed goals should be established with regard to what needs improvement in any areas of the chart selected for analysis.

For example, in the area of individual requisites, it might be decided that money is not a major factor about which something needs to be done in the near term, but that status and opportunity are of great concern to a number of managers at a particular level. Objectives are established in these areas to increase the extent to which such individuals feel needed and heeded and to improve their opportunities. Such objectives will encourage innovation in practices, particularly if managers are encouraged to experiment. Part of the learning process will consist of finding out what doesn't work as well as what does work.

Quite apart from the agreed areas for special analysis by all managers in the group, individual managers should be encouraged to use the whole chart as a reminder of key factors which will have a direct influence on their personal performance and on the performance of other managers. This should hold for all levels of management, but will be particularly pertinent to the middle and lower levels and less experienced managers. Greater achievement, naturally, will come only through skills which are developed into practices which become habits. The emphasis, therefore, is on encouraging each manager to learn what works for him that is good for him and for the organization. He must learn for himself, but he can learn much faster and better with some guidance obtained from the experience of others.

A good part of this guidance will come from the methods which are established to make available to the group what different individuals have learned about their own practices. Just how this is to be done will be a matter of considerable importance to the top manager, and the final decision properly belongs to him. In making a decision, he should keep two important points in mind. First, the reviews should occur at regular intervals, at least three times per year, perhaps more frequently in initial stages of the program. Secondly, his immediate subordinates may on occasion want to meet without his being present to encourage freer expression. He should permit such meetings but should always be briefed later.

Since this book is written primarily for active managers, there should be no apology required for not proposing *the way* to go about putting any such program into action. Such readers know that there is *no one best way,* unless it be their own.

Responsibility for Following Through

It is essential, as previously noted, that the program be recognized as a responsibility of all managers in the group involved. Leadership, in terms of influence and input, should be exerted by all. However, final authority and control must remain with the top manager of the group, which means that he must be an integral and continuing part of the program.

Somebody once said that imagination becomes innovation when you have an original idea and it results in something good. A corollary proposition is that all the good ideas in the world are worthless until they are put into action and cause something to happen. In the field of management practices, there are good ideas being put into action every day which result in something good. Unfortunately, what is for one manager an old idea—so accepted that it has simply become a good habit—is for another manager a unique and original idea on the practice of management. These good ideas which have become good practices must be brought out into the open where others can understand them and adapt them to their own practices.

What is being looked for is when, where, and to what extent the basic organizational factors are influencing the individual factors for good or bad, and vice versa. The individual manager's factors are highly personal and subject to change in degree of importance. In the same way the organization factors, although to some extent the functions of position or organizational structure, can become quite personalized by individuals in position of authority. The top manager must make a management development program his own program because he and his immediate subordinates are the only ones capable of establishing the organization's requisites so that they are in harmony with the individual's requisites. They are in the best position to help enlarge the individual's resources and to exercise their organizational responsibilities so as to conflict minimally with the individual manager's performance of his responsibilities. In this way the results obtained by the individual are optimized in the best interests of the total organization.

It has been wisely observed that only one side gains from domination, that neither side gains from compromise, and that both sides gain only when their interests are integrated or harmonized to produce mutual benefit. Of the fundamentals for the individual and for the organization outlined in the chart, both need what the other has, which sets the stage for this kind of integration.

An emphasis on seeking out what *works* may lead to findings quite different from those produced by an emphasis on what *should work*. Again, it may be found that what works for one manager may not work so well for another. A program which emphasizes the individuality of managers will not be overly concerned with this. The goal, as previously noted, is to recognize and control differences rather than to eliminate them. The entire thrust of the program is to expose managers to the broader experience and perceptions of others rather than to teach them how to think alike.

It should be readily apparent why any such program cannot be handed over to some staff group to develop and conduct and why the top manager and his subordinates must be intimately involved. The doers must be the analysts as well as the goal setters because only they—by improving their understanding of their current practices—can determine how those practices actually *can* be changed, rather than how they theoretically *should* be changed. In this way only can the program retain its orientation to reality and remain concerned with what is being done better and with what is working well in one place which can be expanded.

Seen in this light, the program borrows the strategy and tactics used to put any good ideas into action; that is, it adopts an approach similar to that of other problem-solving efforts of top management, rather than becoming a system for the development of new theories of behavior. To the extent that a particular group of managers improves its comprehension of individual-organization relationships and learns through the interchange of experience how to put into broader practice what seems to produce the best results, its precious time will have been well spent.

An additional point which might be made is that this guide has been written to serve the basic needs of a cohesive group whose leader wants to undertake a program for improved managerial performance. On the other hand, there is no reason why it cannot help anyone seeking to enlarge his understanding of himself as a manager and to improve the effectiveness of his particular subordinates. He must exercise caution only in making sure that his efforts in this direction are in tune with the general style of leadership of his superiors, or at least not directly opposed. In fact, the positive or negative reactions of superiors to such efforts by a manager can help him to determine whether his present working environment is suitable for his continued growth and development as an individual as well as a manager.

Outside Help: Pros and Cons

Should outside help be obtained for the very busy top manager at the outset of a management development program? There is no simple answer. A problem which immediately arises is the difficulty any outsider will have in developing factual information with regard to the practices of any particular group of managers. However, experience indicates that an outsider can be timesaving and productive if he concentrates on helping to uncover what seems to be working and, even more, on developing imaginative ways to make this information meaningfully available to all. This is particularly true in the areas of requisites and resources of accumulated knowledge which may exist outside the group.

It is in the areas of responsibilities and results that the actual practices of any particular group will be found most baffling to the outsider. Even here, however, a particularly keen outside observer or consultant may occasionally be very helpful, particularly if he has no personal axe to grind. He may add a depth of perception or an insight which an insider—involved as he is in day-to-day relations with other managers—finds hard to achieve. However, any person from outside the involved group of managers must be one who can communicate well with, and has the confidence of, the top manager of the group; otherwise not only may results be disappointing, but additional confusion may be introduced into an already complex situation.

measurement and control 6

Politics is the art of looking for trouble, finding it everywhere, diagnosing it wrong and applying unsuitable remedies.

Charles Beard

The Subject of Being Subjective

Politics is a word heard in business corporations more than occasionally. It usually has reference to "high-level" or boardroom activities, with their air of mystery and excitement, or to an individual who is "playing politics," which is a nice way of saying he is advancing himself rather than the business.

Certainly it must be accepted that there can be a considerable amount of political activity in any business organization, if by that we mean the infighting by individuals and groups seeking power or authority, with the attendant "us and them" syndrome. A certain amount of politics is inherent, and quite acceptable, in any self-governing organization, whether in government or business. In business, however, it becomes particularly dangerous when it leads to bureaucracy, because of an overemphasis on agreement with a party line of thinking.

There is a considerable body of evidence that says this kind of situation is most likely to develop in a business organization where subjective opinion is permitted to dominate the decision process, as it so often does in government.

Much evidence also exists that there is too much reliance on subjective evaluations of management personnel in hiring, firing, and promotion practices, even in companies which pride themselves on emphasizing fact over opinion in most decision making. This seems to result, for the most part, from three missing ingredients: time, objective methods for performance measurement, and proper evaluation.

Certainly the time factor for a busy manager is more easily handled if he simply has to spend a bit of time two or three times per year describing how he feels about a subordinate's performance. The lack of objective methods for measurement is usually not of particular concern to any one manager, since all managers are equally affected. The manager similarly feels little pressure from above to evaluate his subordinates more thoroughly, and to give them some feedback, because there is probably no check built into the system to show whether he is performing properly in this area. The only time he really misses constructive evaluation is when he doesn't get it himself from *his* superior.

One of the outgrowths of this kind of situation is the prevalent attitude of top managers that people who particularly like to work with others, and to help them to learn and to grow, should look toward a career in personnel or training or some such staff capacity. It is thought that such individuals obviously do not have sufficient "killer instinct," the "feel for the jugular"; in short, they are not the "tigers" needed for important line management positions.

Good arguments can be made for the need for a number of tigers in any organization, particularly if their natural killer instinct is directed at the competition. However, it is, of course, a fundamental thesis of the kind of program being proposed herein that liking to work with others and liking to help them learn and grow should be an essential part of every manager's job, in his own best interests as well as those of the organization. Without this, management too easily becomes a matter of mystery, mystique, and manipulation. Such management has a poor chance of appealing to the very individuals for whom it is continually crying out—individuals of exceptional intelligence, imagination, courage, character, and integrity.

Almost all managements will say that since the corporation is measured by the bottom line, so must each manager be measured by the bottom line of performance. Since, however, performance in terms of results directly attributable to an individual is frequently hard to identify, the measurement usually becomes more of a value judgment on the way he performs. This value judgment soon crystallizes so that his superior of the moment regards it as a true picture of his performance. A frequent outgrowth of this subjective evaluation is an attempt to describe the individual's personal characteristics. From this, there develops a jargon of buzz words which are generally accepted as meaning good or bad, terms such as "imagination," "initiative," "drive," "aggressiveness," "analytical ability," "resourcefulness," "reaches out for responsibility," and their counterparts.

All too frequently in performance evaluations, specific examples of what a manager actually does are noticeable by their absence. There tends to be a concentration on what the individual is, possesses, or is capable of. Leadership is discussed in terms of *ability* to plan, organize, and follow through, to work effectively with others, to visualize goals and motivate others. Skills are discussed in terms of analytical, communication, and decision-making ability. Personal characteristics such as drive and determination, maturity, emotional stability, resourcefulness, and ingenuity are covered. The trouble with this type of subjective evaluation is fourfold:

1. A manager can possess many desirable characteristics and have most of the desired abilities and still not be a good manager, because he simply doesn't put them all together in a way which produces effective results.

2. Each term tends to mean something different to each person, particularly when there are several levels of experience involved.

3. The norm, or standard, for each characteristic is established by one individual, usually the immediate superior, based upon his own personal experience and attitudes.

4. Particularly in larger organizations and with younger managers, the immediate superior is the only one who can claim to know enough about the subordinate to provide even this limited evaluation.

It is possible to see the type of difficulties described above particularly clearly in the case of a person in his first job of managing other managers. Not only is he almost always, initially, very poorly equipped to manage other managers, but he hardly knows where to begin when the time comes to evaluate them; the chances are that he still isn't at all sure about the real basis on which he himself is being judged. Any reader with experience will have his own long list of such terrible case histories.

This is not to say that there have not been attempts to quantify performance, but too often the limited evidence is relative to subjective terms. Examples are:

Thinking: thoroughness, accuracy, breadth, flexibility, imagination.

Attitude: toward company, job, superiors, others.

Judgment: dealing with people, difficult situations, natural business sense.

Personality: drive, determination, self-discipline.

Ability: skills of analysis, communication, decision making.

Evaluations on such a basis will generally tend to measure degree, and fail to give adequate consideration to the age, experience, position, and situation of the individual. They usually fail to reflect what is considered normal or desirable by more experienced managers, including the top manager. In referring to drive and aggressiveness, "hardheaded" and "hardhearted" will often be considered synonymous. A superficial aggressiveness in dealing with people will be considered a natural corollary of aggressiveness in moving the business ahead.

Most of the behavioral theories and development programs which have been designed to date to help managers out of this dilemma seem to have created a feeling in higher-level managers that they are being threatened by something they don't quite understand, or pretend not to understand because they don't feel a proper sense of control. The resulting lack of full support at the top is quickly felt by others down the line, and suddenly one more attempt at management development has fallen into disrepute.

This further emphasizes the point that unless the top manager of any particular part of an organization can set up his own approach which reflects what *he* wants to accomplish for *his* organization, there will probably never be any broad change for the better in either management practices or the evaluations of such practices. The two are inextricably linked. Though such changes may not be easy, they may very well turn out to be simpler than expected. Complex problems sometimes do have simple solutions.

The Object of Being Objective

The need for more objectivity in evaluations of performance has been only slightly appreciated to date, because single-dimension thinking has led so many organizations to concentrate almost entirely upon the identification and selection of a few managers of highest potential. The evaluation of potential is, of course, one of the most subjective of measurements, because it involves a matter of degree as well as what has not yet happened. However, as pointed out earlier, this seems to have produced reasonably satisfactory results when the organization has been interested only in making sure that its top-rank positions can be filled with high-caliber individuals, developed within the organization or obtained from outside when necessary.

The need for greater objectivity becomes very clear when the objectives are expanded to include the three-dimensional requirements of the organization which, to repeat, are:

1. To provide a broader base of highly competent managers from whom selection can be made for positions of highest responsibility.

2. To provide greater assurance that all managerial positions are filled with individuals competent to help in moving the business ahead.

3. To provide a working environment which ensures for each manager increased resources for his continuing growth, and increased opportunities to use his powers and to achieve his full potential.

Objective evaluation requires a basis of descriptive fact which will help to disclose what an individual has been doing and contributing, as opposed to how he is progressing or learning. It is not a matter of how much he has been soaking up, but how much he has been wringing out of himself. Seen in this way, evaluation becomes a second step of approbation or disapprobation, based upon a more complete and factual definition of accomplishment. Just as confidence in the weapon you are using is nine-tenths of good marksmanship, confidence in the methods used is nine-tenths of good evaluation.

An evaluation based upon what an individual actually does, including how he goes about it, is in fact measuring how he reacts to the situations and challenges with which he is faced. It is seldom that an evaluation thus positions the individual in terms of situations and challenges; instead, the evaluator lapses into a character analysis rather than an exposition of what the individual has done.

This should probably not be too surprising. In his subjective analysis the evaluator is merely slipping into an accepted pattern which he has observed in his superiors. If the evaluation is meant to be favorable, the evaluator will describe in subjective terms the general type of person who is usually considered successful; if the evaluation is meant to be unfavorable, he will use a few phrases usually associated with failure.

The actual performance of, and results obtained by, the manager being evaluated thus tend to be obscured by so much attention to factors such as personality, ability, knowledge, and motivation, no combination of which is ever going to predict what results anyone will actually achieve when faced with a particular situation.

The kind of objective evaluation needed should be designed to avoid most of the dangers of semantic confusion which occur when a manager is reporting to his superior about a subordinate. These two people may have quite different views on what constitutes imagination, drive, aggressiveness, and the like. On the other hand, they can much more quickly agree whether or not a particular result achieved in a particular situation was up to the needs of the situation.

In time, orienting the approach to results achieved tends to bring about an additional advantage: The entire organization's attention is focused on the kind of results being obtained and being expected at different levels of management. This tends to disclose problem areas more readily and, once recognized, they can be more easily corrected. All of this helps to create a working environment in which each manager has the greatest amount of freedom to decide how it will be best for him to go about obtaining a desired result.

Most managers have participated in a session where a relatively junior superior evaluated two managers at the same level, one favorably and the other very unfavorably. Then, when somebody asked how their operations were going, it turned out that the poorly rated manager's business was considerably healthier than that of the well-rated one.

This kind of situation is eliminated when a subjective discussion of a person's strengths and weaknesses is replaced by a descriptive identification of the areas of high and low results. A manager who is keen enough to recognize his own weaknesses (which certainly is part of his responsibility) can frequently achieve a successful result by skillfully using the resources available to him in the strengths of others. In such cases his own knowledge of himself and others proves to be much more important than his superior's impressions of his personal strengths and weaknesses.

Probably the most valuable result of the objective approach, however, is the better identification of high-potential managers. An evaluator and his superior discussing a factual description of results achieved and not achieved are in a good position to appraise a subordinate's true potential for increased responsibilities. This comes about because they know which results areas are most important at the higher levels and how such results relate to what is being achieved at the current level. This permits a reasonable projection of the pattern of current results. Also, it avoids the guessing game of matching up the personal qualities theoretically required at various levels of management, a feat complex enough to baffle a professional psychologist, let alone a couple of amateurs.

At this point, it can properly be asked why this type of results-oriented, objective performance review is so little practiced, particularly in many parts of large organizations. The answer may lie in the increasingly complex organizational structure and the many new and different functions and areas of expertise, both of which make it increasingly difficult to single out the person responsible for a particular result. There seem to be more and more problems which require the efforts of more than one individual. It is frequently difficult even for those involved in such efforts to agree on who was most responsible for a particular result.

One way out of this situation is to fall back upon the tried and true principle of making one individual primarily responsible for results in any particular situation. Then, credit is given or withheld depending entirely upon results. When this is done continuously over a reasonably long period of time, the consistent or inconsistent pattern of an individual's achievements will determine the extent to which his credit is merited.

It is important that factual material be collected continuously and recorded in writing. As mentioned before, this suggests that each manager maintain a diary of some kind. The most useful knowledge which can grow out of this will take the form of patterns which can help (1) to identify and define problem areas for the organization and (2) to provide evidence of consistent performance by an individual. In establishing such written records, it may help to keep things reasonably simple by concentrating on already identified problem areas and on areas of individual performance where there is a recognized need for stronger evidence.

In short, try to *keep it simple,* particularly in initial stages. Also, *keep it positive.* It is a manager's ability to capitalize on his strengths which enables him to produce results, not the absence of weaknesses. This is something which is all too frequently forgotten. The weaknesses which make for a poor manager are often present to some degree in a good manager, but the good manager has learned to keep his weaknesses from getting in the way of his strengths and to use the strengths of others.

Above all, try to *keep an open mind.* There is a natural tendency to see only what one is looking for and to be looking for facts which support an already determined position. The only way to succeed is to keep the ascertaining of facts and the evaluative process separate and distinct until the facts have been determined.

Much of any manager's time is spent administering— not really managing. By applying objective measurements primarily to results he obtains as a manager, with secondary emphasis on his administrative results, the entire evaluation process will be simplified. A good objective rating (R) should equal performance (P) times the strength of the evidence (E) squared, or $R = P \times E^2$. The strength of the evidence is the most important element in an objective measurement.

As in other parts of the business, decisions in the people area will still have to be made without having all the facts one would like to have, no matter how much effort has been made to collect facts. It must be recognized that subjective judgment will always play a part in the evaluation of managers. The purpose is not to eliminate the subjective completely as much as it is to provide a more factual basis upon which judgment can be made. This is why it cannot be overemphasized that fact gathering and the establishment of standards of expectation must precede evaluation, which involves judgment.

Major Missing Ingredients

In current attempts at measurement and control, the most important missing ingredient is time. The lack of time probably causes more unwanted results than any other single factor. Without more time devoted to improving the practices of each manager, from top to bottom, very little improvement will ever be achieved. This means that the necessary time must somehow be found and must be used efficiently. This will present a personal challenge to each manager which only he can resolve.

The next most important missing ingredient is undoubtedly factual measurements of what each manager has done which can be used as a basis for decision and control. By this is meant measurements which are better understood by both the evaluator and the individual being evaluated than those in general use today. The current practice is to judge managers primarily on "performance," that is, on the basis of a personal value judgment made by one superior. When actual performance can't be adequately measured, it is just too easy for a manager who is handling his people poorly to place the blame on them, particularly if he is a manager who performs well in other areas. In most companies an individual who has the confidence of his superiors can freely mishandle his subordinate managers; only when the subordinates are driven to the point of revolt will his weakness become of concern to his superiors.

A third major missing ingredient is an effective review of performance. Most managers at all levels are unwilling to clarify the kind and level of performance they are looking for. Since evaluation is based upon so many subjective factors, they consider it a highly personal matter.

Some managers dislike performance reviews with subordinates because they don't want to make up their minds until the time comes to fire or promote, others because they are unconsciously embarrassed by the idea of discussing with a subordinate a subject they consider to be highly personal.

Any solution to this problem undoubtedly requires that the organization adopt the same sense of commitment *toward* subordinates that it expects *from* them. This two-way commitment is not a strange idea, for it is something already done in most companies with a few high-potential individuals marked for special attention. The top management group in such companies may insist that they make no promises to anybody, and this is usually true. However, they do make words, even adding music when necessary, to help hold such a marked individual. Those who have not had such effective performance reviews can easily become eager to avoid mistakes and play it safe, or to seek a new employer who, at least while hiring them, will make all sorts of nice, ego-massaging words.

Anyone who realistically attempts to provide a management development program with those required ingredients (time, adequate measurements of performance, and effective performance reviews) is bound to be impressed by the necessity for each manager to fit himself to his particular job in his own way. The choice is whether to let him find his own way entirely or to work with him in a way which exposes him to the broader experiences of others. If left to his own devices, his actual practices may remain largely unknown to his superior and may or may not be in the best interests of the organization. By working together in a constructive way, both the superior and subordinate are in a better position to learn what seems to work best. Far from interpreting his superior's interest as an intrusion on his own prerogatives, the subordinate is much more likely to view it as an indication that he is not just an interchangeable part.

Interchangeability of managers is generally recognized as a valid need in large organizations, and every manager must to some extent accept its validity. However, when the better and younger manager in particular feels, rightly or wrongly, that he is *only* a replaceable part, he may also feel that his identity, if not his actual integrity, is threatened. The key to a proper relationship in this delicate area of people handling is consistency on the part of the superior. Occasional intrusion can be upsetting; consistent involvement can be reassuring and, when conducted on a mutual learning basis, usually provides added stimulation to the subordinate.

Establishing Performance Expectations

To some sound and forceful thinkers in management, the idea of establishing any form of performance expectations as part of the basis for individual evaluations is anathema. To them, it seems to smack too much of rigid adherence to a system of rules. These same individuals, on the other hand, will in all other aspects of their operations pride themselves on emphasizing that what you know is more important than what you think, that fact holds sway over opinion in every decision.

Give such a manager a checklist of important factors in the background of recent graduates applying for a starting position in the management program and he will ignore it and say that the only important thing is whether, after an hour's interview, he feels he would like a person to be working for him. Provide him with a list of the performance objectives generally agreed to be most important at a particular level of management and he will ignore it as a basis for evaluation and say he will decide how good the individual is the next time he has to make a choice for promotion.

He looks for self-directed, very ambitious, highly motivated individuals, places them in positions where they can learn and develop, and believes that the better ones will "float to the top." He assumes that these better managers will maintain their self-motivation and that their superior performance will lead to satisfaction on the job. So long as *his* superiors are looking to him for only an occasional manager capable of handling higher responsibilities, this practice works reasonably well. With the majority of his subordinates, he waits patiently for an essential weakness to develop and allows it to grow to the point where it blocks promotion. Not many enjoy working for him, and turnover is high. He belongs to another age.

A fallacy in postponing decisions about the individual performance of a particular group of managers until the need arises to promote somebody is the assumption that the "best" will still be around at that time. The chances are great, of course, that between promotions a number of fine development prospects will leave the organization voluntarily because they don't know where they stand or are not getting any positive signals.

One might think that their immediate superior, or his superiors, would be concerned about losing people who seemed quite competent. Occasionally, indeed, one of those lost who had succeeded in making a favorable impression up the line may cause a brief flurry of excitement about what must be done to assure that the organization does not lose such good people in the future. However, it is all too easy to avoid personal responsibility by placing it on somebody else or by blaming the departee, who "just wasn't thinking straight." Negative comments about the individual which had surprisingly not surfaced previously will then begin to be heard so that any feeling of guilt about losing a good man soon disappears.

There are four major purposes to be served by the establishment of generally accepted expectations of performance for various managerial positions, from the lowest through the middle ranks:

1. Identifying and understanding the critical combination of abilities needed to perform the particular job, so that performance can be measured by significant evidence of these abilities in what an individual actually does.

2. Identifying the areas where more factual evidence is needed and providing additional opportunities for learning and development in these areas.

3. Using this information on a continuing daily basis to provide a subordinate with a better understanding of what is expected at different stages of personal development, as well as on occasions of performance-development reviews.

4. Helping to identify those promising individuals who are best qualified to assume increasingly important assignments.

Without any kind of established expectations for performance against which a manager at a certain level can be measured, there is simply no way of measuring the 80 percent of managers who fall in the gray area, who seem to be neither outstanding nor worthless. No well-run business would dispense with accepted norms for factory operations or sales operations or return on capital, but when it comes to the return on human resources it is a different matter. The important missing essential is the ability to provide managers at all levels with objective people data for decision and control.

At present, the fund of such data is not even remotely comparable to the mass of factual information taken for granted in other areas of a business. When managers who would like to improve this situation in their organization look for help, they find it is offered primarily by theorists who have ideas only on what *should* be. It is characteristic of a good manager in such cases to make his own assumptions and to have his own opinions, in the absence of any hard facts. There is nothing sadder than to see a young line manager or a staff service manager trying to convince a fairly senior line manager on the basis of how strongly he feels or thinks, rather than on the basis of what he knows.

In being objective, the major concern is whether something *is* or *is not*, whether somebody *does* or *does not* do something or produce something. This then gets reflected in evaluative terms such as "equal–*or* not equal–to job" and "ready–*or* not ready–for greater responsibility," and in such statements as "The evidence is sufficient–*or* not sufficient–that manager X has–*or* lacks–superior potential." It simply is not possible to obtain this kind of objectivity without standards of expectation. It is possible for two managers to disagree that an individual is equal to his job if there is no agreement on the results which somebody equal to the job should be achieving. In short, without performance expectations, it is practically impossible to understand the relevance of objective evidence and two managers can interpret those same facts and come up with different conclusions.

In objective evaluation the process is one of inductive reasoning, that is, reasoning from the specific to the general. The dangers, of course, arise from trying to generalize on the basis of too few facts or too great an assortment of unrelated facts. Agreement with regard to expectations for the key performance areas helps to make certain facts more pertinent and more valuable. This is especially true when the objective of the process is to measure not only individual performance and achievement, but achievement in broader areas, such as a particular level of the organization.

To be most useful, any evaluation process should take into consideration different individual rates for the kind of learning which produces results, and the difference in learning situations. This in itself requires norms, or standards, of expectation. For example, should a business school graduate be expected to make quicker progress in his first two or three years as a manager than a person with a liberal arts degree? Unless there is agreement on whether or not this is to be expected, evaluations will reflect differences in the opinions and attitudes of individual evaluators.

The objective approach removes such purely personal opinion. An analysis of the facts based upon the organization's experience with managers of both collegiate backgrounds can determine whether there is indeed a difference in initial results obtained by the two groups.

Any differences that exist should, of course, then be reflected in different expectations for each group.

To make this more palatable, perhaps it should be compared to par in golf. Without a par, there would be no way of knowing what is expected and no thrill in a birdie or disappointment in a bogey. Furthermore, there would be no way of handicapping the players to indicate which ones have the consistently better games. Therefore, the ability to predict the performance of any player or group of players would be limited. Having a par encourages the good golfer to try to do better. Similarly, the good manager who is aware of the accepted expectations for his job will knock himself out trying to surpass them.

On the other hand, undesirable results occur when agreement on managerial expectations is lacking. A perfect example of this frequently occurs when a young manager receives his first promotion and a new title. He may find to his disappointment that his superiors appear to expect little more of him, except perhaps in quantity, than they did before. It is possible to witness a whole series of lower-level managers go through a slump when this recurs repeatedly in some area of the organization.

This might be a good point at which to admit that if each junior or middle manager could be assured of working directly for an experienced senior manager with a track record for developing other managers, there would be much less need for a management development program such as this. We all know managers—but unfortunately too few of them—who are fond of saying that the year or two they spent working for old so and so were worth their right arm.

However, most younger managers, in particular, are

working directly for superiors whose performance in developing good managers is highly questionable; it is awareness of this fact that calls for a management development program. The worst situation of all, of course, occurs when young management prospects, who are in their potentially most formative period, are placed under the responsibility of the most junior, or least able, managers because that is where they fit on the organization chart.

The most potent argument for accepted expectations of performance is, of course, the alternative, which is to have as many different expectations as there are managers in the organization. Some of these will be subjective and some objective; some will be unrealistically high and some unrealistically low, depending upon the ability and experience of the manager and his basic attitude toward the ability of others. There is considerable evidence that managers with superior performance tend to have higher expectations for their subordinates than do average or inferior managers. Since most organizations have only a minority of their managers in the superior category, the natural result is an average expectancy which is probably lower than desirable.

Another great advantage of the use of accepted expectations of performance will be seen when the subjects of constructive feedback and corrective action are considered in Chapter 7. Developing constructive feedback and taking corrective action are jobs which come naturally to very few managers, and even they can be more effective when provided with some guidance. Experience has shown that subjectively oriented critiques, which tend to be personalized value judgments, put the person on the defensive or challenge his opinion of himself so that his mind is often closed to what is being said.

On the other hand, objective evaluations which are based upon accepted performance expectations provide an entirely different environment for feedback and corrective action. It is possible to conduct a review of problems or opportunities faced and results achieved over a four- to six-month period in a way which places the burden of rating the person's performance on the person himself. This serves to obtain clear agreement on the areas in which effort must be concentrated in the future.

In determining what facts are really needed, simultaneous consideration should be given to how these are to be obtained and how they will be used as the basis for evaluation. In addition, to help in identifying and selecting individuals of "highest potential" for special programming, a deliberate agreement should be reached among key managers on (1) what it is that must be known about a developing manager, and (2) at what point in his career pertinent events can be expected to occur.

The chart of fundamentals can serve as a useful tool in this regard. (See the end of Chapter 4.) However, there is a pitfall in the use of such a comprehensive chart: It may appear that what is being sought is the well-rounded manager for all managerial positions. The fact is that good managers often are, like the world, not round but a little egg-shaped. Time and various forces have flattened (and sharpened) them a bit in certain places, and they are a bit rounder (or smoother) in certain areas than in others.

Any intelligent use of the chart requires a selection from it of those factors which are most important to a particular level and specific part of the total corporate organization. Obviously, in the relative importance of various factors there will be differences between a staff or service department and a line management department, or, perhaps, between manufacturing and sales. The proper selection of factors is something which can be done only by those who are initiating the program for improvement, that is, the top manager concerned and his immediate subordinates. In selecting the most important factors for measurement, they must keep in mind the purposes of the program. These are to produce more and better results by promoting throughout the organization those practices which will best improve each manager's self-development and ability to work effectively with others.

Concentrated effort must be made to obtain the facts that really need to be known, not what someone would like to know. This body of necessary factual information should be determined for each level and function of management. It should start with what really must be known about those being recruited for starting positions in a management development program and continue through the middle management levels. What must be known is the critical combination of abilities required to optimize results expected at any one level, and there must be significant evidence of what an individual *does* which is directly the result of the use of these abilities. This is also what must be known to provide each manager, particularly in his younger and most formative periods, with the basis for a better understanding of what is expected of him at different stages in his development.

To assist in clarifying the above points, the following exhibits suggest the kinds of performance which might be looked for in a college recruit for management development (Exhibit 1), an employee on his first managerial assignment (Exhibit 2), and a person in a key middle management position (Exhibit 3). Exhibit 4 is a sample of a summary appraisal form which might be used by the rater and retained in the confidential files of the department head to assist in assessment of the department's strengths and forward manpower planning. Exhibit 5 is a form for a recap summary which might be kept under lock and key by the top manager of the department or division.

EXHIBIT 1. PROFILE OF THE OUTSTANDING CANDIDATE FOR MANAGEMENT.

College recruits for management development programs, like managers themselves, include many different types, and there is ample room for individual style. In appraising the candidate, his possession of the traditional characteristics and abilities* is less important than *evidence* of what he has been able to do with them to date. The outstanding candidate in general can significantly *demonstrate* that he has or is rapidly developing the following characteristics and abilities in his areas of primary interest. He (or she):

1. Is strongly motivated to achieve excellence and has demonstrated a consistent ability to do so.
2. Has a curious, probing mind and can use it to generate original ideas and to reach well-reasoned conclusions.
3. Is a resourceful self-teacher who has learned from experiences to make himself (or herself) as effective as possible.
4. Has tended to seek a role as a leader, effectively setting goals and motivating others, and maintaining a strong sense of responsibility for results.
5. Thinks a problem through, decides, takes action, and stays involved.
6. In conversation, is responsive and demonstrates clarity of thinking and persuasiveness.
7. Has demonstrated a scope of interests and abilities which provide an adequate basis for a genuine and lasting interest in the type of work applied for.

*The traditional characteristics and abilities sought in a candidate have been defined as analytical ability, communication skills, ability to work with others, leadership, resourcefulness and ingenuity, decision making, and drive and determination in following through.

EXHIBIT 2. PERFORMANCE EXPECTATIONS FOR THE MANAGEMENT INITIATE.

THINKS
He identifies and understands problems and reaches thoroughly substantiated, well-reasoned conclusions which lead to action.

LEARNS
He faces new situations with confidence. He works hard at maximizing his personal effectiveness, gains insights from experiences, and doesn't repeat mistakes or wait to be told.

INNOVATES
He looks for better ways and generates good, practicable ideas which contribute not only to his assigned area of responsibility but to other areas of the organization's activities.

COMMUNICATES
He speaks concisely, writes clearly and persuasively, and responds with flexibility to the ideas of others. His attempts to communicate always reflect his appreciation of the importance of other people's time.

LEADS
He assumes a leading role, sets high goals, and effectively motivates others to get results.

IDENTIFIES
He identifies with the organization's goals; relates well to those below, around, and above him; and approaches his responsibilities in a positive, businesslike manner.

PRODUCES
He consistently turns out a high volume of excellent work on time.

EXHIBIT 3. PERFORMANCE EXPECTATIONS FOR THE KEY MIDDLE MANAGER.

The manager should be measured objectively on the strength of the evidence that he does the following things directly related to responsibilities and results. Particular attention should be given to any special handling which may be required to provide stronger evidence on any of the following points by the time of his next evaluation.

INITIATES

1. Identifies significant problems, understands their causes, and comes up with ideas which are well supported and lead to action designed to move the business ahead.
2. Thinks decisively and resourcefully of new approaches to a particularly difficult problem.
3. Takes the initiative in setting high goals and in motivating others to attack and solve problems.
4. Assumes the primary responsibility for his own development and works hard at maximizing his strengths while correcting areas of weakness.

INFLUENCES

1. Appreciates the importance of facts in reducing the number of decisions which must be made on judgment alone.
2. Presents a persuasive oral point of view as well as concise and accurate written work.
3. Deals flexibly with people and with difficult situations in a way which inspires the respect of others.
4. Provides a proper learning environment for subordinates, in which they have ample opportunity to utilize strengths and to recognize and correct weaknesses.

ADMINISTERS

1. Produces excellent work under pressure planning ahead and staying on top of a broad range of activities through good personal organization of time and work load.
2. Utilizes the help and advice of other departments to increase his leverage in executing plans; delegates responsibility without losing a deep sense of personal responsibility.

EXHIBIT 3. (CONT.)

3. Makes the system work for him in the execution, control, and subsequent evaluation of agreed-upon projects.

ACHIEVES RESULTS

1. Moves the business ahead.
2. Develops others.
3. Advances himself.

EXHIBIT 4. A SUMMARY APPRAISAL FORM

Personal and Confidential
(original only—no copies)

Name _____

Position _____

Time in position_____

Time with company_____

Circle the number of the statement below
which best describes your overall appraisal
of this person at this time.

DESCRIPTION

1. Outstanding in ability to learn, to develop, and to contribute to the thinking of the business.

2. Developing well, with clear potential for additional responsibilities in the future.

3. Good performance on broad range of current job responsibilities, but potential for additional responsibilities still in question.

4. Not yet handling broad range of current job responsibilities but still developing.

5. Performance definitely not up to requirements of position; needs to be replaced.

EXHIBIT 4. (CONT.)

	Name	Position	Date
Evaluated by	_____	_____	_____
Concurrence by	_____	_____	_____

NOTE: These appraisals will be made twice per year (in January and July) to assist in forward manpower planning and to provide an overall "strength report" in terms of how people are developing at various levels in the organization.

EXHIBIT 5. A FORM FOR A MANPOWER-PLANNING SUMMARY

Secret
(original only)

Department or division _____   Date _____

MANAGER'S CURRENT ASSESSMENT	STARTING POSITION	SECOND LEVEL	THIRD LEVEL	FOURTH LEVEL
A. *Most promising* Excellent prospect for additional responsibilities. Possible months until ready shown in ( ) after name.				
B. *Basically satisfactory* Continuing to develop and performing up to basic requirements of current job.				
C. *Doubtful* Not developing up to basic requirements of current job. Decision may be needed before next review in six months.				
D. *Replace* Performance on current job not satisfactory considering time in position.				

any additional comments

Signature _____

(Manager)

maximizing
the practices
that work   7

What works is infinitely preferable to what doesn't work.

Benjamin Franklin

Previous chapters have concentrated upon equating individual and organization fundamentals and orienting a management development program to reality by concentrating attention on results to be achieved. It has been emphasized that in many management situations there may be a number of different actions which can achieve the same results. Experience indicates that, when in doubt, the best action is probably the one which will generate the most enthusiasm among those who are involved.

The basic result desired of a management development program is to get all managers to react more flexibly and more positively to what all of them have learned so that they will maximize the practices that work best. This leads inevitably to the all-important subjects of constructive feedback and corrective action, without which no controlled changes can take place.

Constructive Feedback

Since so much attention in previous chapters has been devoted to the importance of what *is*, this discussion must emphasize the fact that feedback is concerned with people and situations not as they *are* but as they are *perceived* to be. Each manager sees a situation or a person in his own unique way, and his perceptions are often quite different from those of others. The goal, of course, is to make sure that a perception is not a deception and, in this way, to bring all the perceptions closer together.

One of the first things to get straight is the perception related to learning, because learning is something a manager must continue to do throughout his career unless he is to stop growing. One of the great problems with many development programs, particularly for younger managers, is that they nourish the idea, sometimes unconsciously, that it is somebody else's job to teach rather than the individual's job to learn for himself. Just as the organization internally generates its own development, so it must rely on managers who are able to generate their own development.

It is universally accepted that learning involves how *not* to do something, learned from one's own mistakes and those of others, as well as how to do something successfully. It cannot be denied that there is something which can be learned from every job and every situation and from others with whom one works. This is frequently interpreted as meaning that practically everything to be learned about the job must be learned on the job. However, when a manager in any program for improvement is faced with a new situation it is desirable to have a resource available where he can learn what similar situations have occurred in the past, what was done, and how successful the results were. Such a learning resource would never tell him automatically what to do, but would provide him with a broader experience upon which to base his decision.

That might be termed a good example of guiding an individual to achieve a better end result for the organization while simultaneously assisting him in his own personal learning process. It would be hard to argue that this is not an improvement over simply leaving the individual to his own devices and mistakes, based upon his own limited experience.

Constructive feedback is thus seen to have the following specific objectives:

1. To provide broad exposure for accumulated experience with regard to what works, with the flow of such information directed both upward and downward.

2. To provide this experience in imaginative and meaningful ways which accelerate the growth of an individual's learning process and his ability to produce results which are of benefit to the organization. Both the individual and the organization should be the beneficiaries when feedback is constructive.

It will be noted that there is no mention above of feedback in connection with telling a subordinate what you think of him. That is considered to be not constructive feedback but corrective action and should not be handled as a part of the feedback process. In fact, as discussed later, it is better to avoid that kind of corrective action. The point is to avoid associating either evaluation or feedback with something you *do to* a subordinate. Constructive feedback should automatically connote a two-way communication and learning process. If a superior is *telling* a subordinate about the subordinate's weaknesses, it is quite unlikely that the subordinate will reciprocate by describing the weaknesses he perceives in the superior, unless he has already made up his mind about leaving.

Constructive feedback, as defined here, is really the creation of a working environment in which the resources of the organization, in terms of its total managerial experience, are made meaningfully available to the individual manager. Additionally, the best practices of managers at specific levels are shared in a way which maximizes the end results obtained by each individual and the organization.

This becomes increasingly important as corporate organizations become divisionalized or multinational. Just as the multinational corporation can capitalize on heavy research costs by finding new markets for the products of this research, so the heavy costs of accumulated managerial experience can be exploited by finding new ways to spread this experience over a broader base of managers. Policies, principles, and procedures cannot by themselves be expected to fill the need. Constructive feedback, in the final analysis, will flourish best in an environment in which managers effectively relate to their specific jobs and to each other and show willingness to develop a two-way form of communication concerning what works.

Corrective Action

It is important, at the outset, to recognize that "corrective action" as discussed here is not disciplinary in the usual sense, except when a manager needs to be terminated. In all other instances corrective action is assumed to mean the positive process of trying to make something different happen which will produce a higher level of achievement for the individual and the organization. As such, it requires the same application of imagination that is needed in any other activity of the business where an accepted way of thinking is to be changed. A classic example of poor corrective action is a confrontation between superior and subordinate in which:

1. The problem is not spelled out clearly.
2. The problem has been allowed to exist too long before any discussion.
3. There is no corroboration from a higher level.
4. The atmosphere of the discussion is threatening.

In the above approach, the chances for improvement are slight and there is a danger that a personality conflict may develop.

A more imaginative confrontation might proceed along the following lines:

1. The problem is viewed as a specific thing which is happening and which is important to the individual and the organization.
2. The superior seeks an approach which is non-threatening.

3. The discussion is open-minded, and ideas are sought from the subordinate so that corrective action will be self-motivated.

When this more imaginative kind of corrective action is undertaken, it will usually be found that both the superior and the subordinate are stimulated to learn something from the discussion. From this, both managers are imbued with a greater awareness of the subordinate's true value and the changes which are most likely to produce better results.

Sometimes it is the subordinate who approaches the superior. If he does so on a matter of advancing himself rather than the business, he will probably find the sharing of ideas to be much more limited. The young, ambitious manager might, in the absence of much positive feedback or suggestions on needed corrective action, take an opportunity to ask his superior to identify those areas of his performance whose improvement would increase his chances of rapid advancement. If he does, he should not be surprised or dismayed to receive a reply along the lines of "You're a smart guy: Figure it out for yourself." However, if the subordinate should instead open a discussion on various options available in an upcoming decision designed to advance his part of the business, he might find himself the recipient of more help than he really was seeking.

In retrospect, then, one of the most important keys to improved managerial performance is a much greater awareness of what corrective action should encompass and of the dangers and pitfalls which exist in most current corrective processes. This enlarged awareness comes from a greater appreciation for the fact that managers at all levels are seeking from the organization or department basically the same satisfactions and rewards:

1. An environment in which they can achieve opportunity, status, and money.

2. An environment in which they can enlarge their knowledge, imagination, and reason and thereby improve the performance of their responsibilities to initiate, influence, and administer.

3. An environment in which they can contribute through an increasing ability to move the business ahead, develop others, and advance themselves.

Such an organizational environment is created by the ways in which managers actually relate to their specific jobs and to each other. There can be no such entity as an impersonal organization, except on paper. There can only be managers who act impersonally. There can be no such entity as a dynamic organization unless the managers are dynamic.

One of the biggest problems confronting a manager in most large organizations is that in a decision situation he seldom sees anybody above his immediate superior face to face. This has obvious advantages in terms of efficient use of time, but it can be overdone to the point where it hurts both the individual and the organization. It hurts by limiting the manager's opportunity to obtain insights into the pattern of thinking of a boss' superior. It also hurts by tending to place the entire burden of evaluation and corrective action on one immediate superior.

The importance of that point is recognized by the following fact: An individual who has been identified as possessing high potential for increased responsibilities will frequently receive such exposure up the line, thus helping his development and, incidentally, helping to make the prophecy of high potential self-realizing. Such exposure is equally important for all managers. The demands of time can still be met, since such meetings with other superiors do not have to be on a daily or even weekly basis. In other words, to encourage individual initiative down the line, the management up the line must exercise a little initiative itself.

Corrective action of any sort also conflicts directly with the desire of every busy manager to reduce talking time and to increase the amount of written communication. If the thinking in business were always rational and decisions logical, perhaps communication could be almost 100 percent in the written form. Unfortunately, this is not so, and the problem is further confounded by the previously noted practical need to forgo complete candidness at times.

Corrective action will usually require personal, face-to-face communication. When two people are talking, and each is listening, there can be real understanding. With such understanding there develops the kind of mutual trust which always lies at the bottom of the most effective working relationships. Some superiors argue that leaving a subordinate to his own devices, with a minimum of contact, is a sign of trust and confidence, forgetting that he can all too easily interpret this, rightly or wrongly, as an indication that the superior couldn't care less.

Whereas constructive feedback can involve any number of superiors, subordinates, and peers, corrective action almost always involves a one-to-one situation of superior and subordinate. This is where we once again see the great advantage in objectifying and defining experience to delineate what is actually being done and what is happening as a result. This type of objective review of the situation helps the individual who must undergo correction to better understand for himself what needs to be done. Then, based upon his knowledge of himself, he can better figure out how he should go about doing it. When the subordinate thus understands what is expected of him and what he expects of himself, he can proceed with confidence.

Quite frequently the current evaluation practices will include a statement by the evaluator on what he thinks needs to be done by the individual being rated. Where subjective ratings are involved, the rater frequently acts like an amateur psychologist and, most of the time, nothing much happens after all is said and done, usually because more is said than done. Even where more objective ratings are obtained by means of more specific, factual supporting evidence, there is always a tendency for the rater to tell the individual what to do. This is not only trying to do his job for him, but it is "telling and teaching" rather than putting the material in front of him and guiding him in a way which helps him to learn and see for himself.

The superior has every right to expect and insist that any subordinate assume primary responsibility for his own development. He should further expect any subordinate to understand, and respect, the organization's goals and objectives and the policies, procedures, and principles needed for their achievement. He should be looking to the subordinate for contributions and a complete sense of personal responsibility for the area assigned.

In this connection, one of the best ways to teach responsibility is to give a subordinate a job that isn't going to get done if he doesn't do what he needs to, and—barring complications—to leave him free to figure out how to do it and to get it done. One of the very best places to use this method is in the area of self-development. If, in addition, the subordinate is provided with better access to those broader experiences of others that will enlarge his personal resources and improve his performance, the superior may be pleasantly surprised. He may find that he has gone a long way toward satisfying the subordinate's needs, minimizing conflicts, avoiding syndromes, and building a positive attitude.

What we are trying to avoid here is the conflict which frequently occurs between individual responsibility and organizational authority. If a superior tells a subordinate "You are responsible for your own development" and then uses his authority to tell the subordinate how to go about it, he is creating a completely unnecessary conflict.

Too much autocratic or authoritarian behavior on a consistent basis causes too much arbitrariness, which in turn is responsible for much unnecessary conflict. Of all the factors on the chart of fundamentals, it will probably be generally agreed that conflict between organization and individual is potentially greatest in the exercise of responsibilities. The organization must have leadership, authority, and controls. The individual's responsibilities are initiating, influencing, and administering. The opposition of these responsibilities of the individual and the organization creates the most dangerous area of relationships, and it is where personality clashes develop and corrective action is most often needed.

If conflicts in this area are not anticipated and minimized, the necessary results desired of the individual will suffer. If emphasis is placed upon optimizing the abilities of each manager to achieve the individual results which are needed, the organization's results of profits, growth, and perpetuation will be optimized.

The truly good manager recognizes all this and concentrates on seeking opportunities, and rewards, for those who are not particularly adept at advancing themselves but are particularly good at advancing the business. For example, the research head may have a manager who is quite incapable of handling more than two assistants but is in a more valuable position, and paid more, than another research manager with a much larger group reporting to him. An engineering head who has appointed a manager to spend a year on a solo project to enlarge the capacity of a key piece of equipment may find that the dollar rewards from this solo effort are greater than those from the combined contributions of all his other managers.

It is surprising how frequently an organization's leaders are expressing the need for more individual initiative while its managers are crying out for the same thing. This is another area where conflicts can arise and corrective action is often needed. "Initiative" in its best sense does not mean just starting something, but includes persevering until the act is accomplished. Initiative occurs most frequently in an environment which not only permits but encourages individual managers to exercise it.

Such freedom to exercise initiative does not mean unilateral freedom to *act*; it should mean absolute freedom to *think* and to *decide* and encouragement to act. Good managers must, therefore, not only be receptive to new ideas or thinking, they must be receptive to change when it is needed.

"Initiative" could properly be termed leadership at

the individual level regardless of organizational position. It can often conflict with organization leadership, which should be, as indicated on the chart, primarily confined to overall goals, determination of priorities, and allocation of resources. The initiative of managers can be greatly stimulated by their better understanding of these overall goals, priorities, and available resources. This is a sensitive area where secrecy may sometimes be required.

The point is that corrective action does not consist of telling an individual he must exert more initiative. It involves guiding him to perceive a better direction for his initiative, where it is most likely to be acted upon because it does not conflict with the goals, priorities, and available resources of the organization.

Translating Thinking into Doing

New ideas need new decisions in order to be translated into action. In order to translate the proposed way of thinking into a way of doing, it will help to keep certain concepts and objectives in mind. Analysis of the thinking outlined in the previous chapters will show that it involves three main concepts about management development:

1. The needs of the manager and those of the organization can be equated in terms of specific requisites, resources, responsibilities, and results—the Four R's of the management equation.

2. A manager's achievement level, in terms of results, is optimized by harmonizing requisites, improving and enlarging resources, and minimizing conflicts in responsibilities.

3. The total organization's achievement level, in terms of results, is optimized by fully capitalizing on

the differing strengths of individual managers. This is done by finding imaginative ways for all managers to be exposed to the most effective practices which develop from these individual strengths.

Based upon these concepts, a decision can be made to undertake a management development program that is oriented to reality and has three clear objectives, which are mutually supporting:

1. To provide a broader base of highly competent managers from among whom selection can be made for positions of highest responsibility.

2. To provide greater assurance that all managerial positions at all levels will be filled with individuals competent to help in moving the business ahead.

3. To provide a working environment which will ensure for each manager increased resources for his continuing growth and increased opportunities to use his powers and to achieve his full potential.

In taking action, following such a decision, it should be kept in mind that there is no one method which will suit the differing styles of leadership or immediate needs of all parts of an organization. The point to remember is that the burden to develop strengths should be on the manager and the burden to maximize the effectiveness of these strengths should be on his superiors.

The specific method to be followed in any particular cohesive part of the organization can therefore best be determined by the top manager and his immediate subordinates. They are the ones in the best position to determine (1) what parts of the basic equation chart need priority attention at a particular time and (2) how to collect information broadly. In weighing various alternative approaches, the approach to select is the one with the best chance of achieving not just one, but all three, of the objectives of the program, as listed above.

In practice, the top manager can involve his entire management group and can utilize staff help and/or outside consultants, but he himself must play a key role on a continuing basis. Only in this way, experience clearly indicates, can he make sure that his program stays on the tracks and that the best practices become broadly established throughout his organization.

In measuring effectiveness of a development program, in terms of both individual and organization, it will be found that the new ideas, new decisions, and new actions which help most to achieve results are also what help most to identify the real achievers. The objective, or factual, approach places emphasis on what an individual *does* and on *what happens* which improves the results he obtains that benefit both himself and the organization.

In the last analysis, a realistic approach to management development requires the application to the human resources of the organization of that sound and forceful thinking common to most other aspects of operations. For example, no organization would think of not trying to capitalize fully on the large investments usually associated with research and development. However, there is ample evidence from many sources that practically no organization, even among the very best managed, has even begun to capitalize fully on its tremendous investment in managerial experience.

The time for decision, the time for action, is now.